Praise for pre ___

How Good People Make Tough Choices
"At a time when moral questions tend to be argued with more heat than light, Kidder offers practical guidelines for a coherent and mindful approach to ethical dilemmas. . . . A brilliant and practical analysis that squarely faces all the issues and can be grasped by the thoughtful nonspecialist."
—Kirkus Reviews

"A thought-provoking guide to enlightened and progressive personal behavior."
—Jimmy Carter

Moral Courage
"Kidder links sophisticated theory and research with colorful, sometimes gripping examples of people displaying the 'courage to be moral' despite potential loss of security, wealth, friendships, and/or freedom. This book, like one candle in the darkness, belongs in every place of learning—and every library."
—Library Journal

"*Moral Courage* is a wonderful book—lively, thoughtful, and practical. It is grounded in careful research, explained with clear analysis, and enlivened by great, real-life stories."
—Bob Abernethy, executive editor of *Religion & Ethics Newsweekly* on PBS

Also by Rushworth M. Kidder

Dylan Thomas: The Country of the Spirit

E. E. Cummings: An Introduction to the Poetry

An Agenda for the 21st Century

Reinventing the Future:
Global Goals for the 21st Century

In the Backyards of Our Lives

Heartland Ethics:
Voices from the American Midwest
(editor)

Shared Values for a Troubled World:
Conversations with Men and Women of Conscience

How Good People Make Tough Choices:
Resolving the Dilemmas of Ethical Living

Moral Courage:
Taking Action When Your Values Are Put to the Test

The Ethics Recession

Reflections on the Moral Underpinnings of the Current Economic Crisis

Rushworth M. Kidder

Institute for Global Ethics
Rockland, Maine • London • Vancouver

The chapters in this book originally appeared during 2007, 2008, and 2009 in *Ethics Newsline®,* an electronic newsletter published weekly by the Institute for Global Ethics (www.globalethics.org) and made possible through generous support from Accenture, Deloitte LLC, Northrop Grumman, the Richard Lounsbery Foundation, The J. M. Smucker Company, Weyerhaeuser, and the members and friends of the Institute.

First edition published 2009
Cover design by Carol Gillette

The Library of Congress has catalogued this book as follows:
The ethics recession: reflections on the moral underpinnings of the current economic recession / Rushworth M. Kidder

ISBN-10:   0-615-27535-4
ISBN-13:   978-0-615-27535-2

Contents

III
Why Integrity Matters

Introduction

A s this book goes to press, the news is awash with reports on the duplicities of Bernard Madoff, the financial trader whose activities allegedly created the world's largest Ponzi scheme and cost his clients some $50 billion. Investigative stories also are beginning to trickle in about the broader genesis of the financial crisis, probing such suspect practices as the devil-may-care loan making that made Washington Mutual the nation's largest savings and loan bank — and the largest bank failure in American history. Attention is also turning to the apparent laxity of regulators, corporate leaders, and members of Congress in failing to scotch the lending epidemic while it was still in its infancy. Through it all, one thing is becoming clear: With every passing day, this crisis is moving from questions of numbers and money to questions of integrity and identity. What started as a financial recession has been revealed as an ethics recession.

This book examines this new variety of recession. It looks at the collapse of ethics and the failures of moral courage that finally became evident in the financial numbers. It contemplates (among other things) the millions of little gray lies that happened in tiny conference rooms in banks across

America. These lies helped prospective borrowers and mortgage lenders inflate applicants' reported resources in order to qualify for loans that, in many cases, proved un-repayable. As these lies grew bigger and blacker, they escaped from the conference rooms into the executive suite, where they were bundled into glitteringly tempting derivatives and sold to other executives who never had understood them and didn't really want to.

This is a book about the moral underpinnings of the current crisis. I've described it as a series of "Reflections," since it comprises thirty columns that were penned as the crisis was unfolding. Published largely in 2008, with some from the latter half of 2007 and early 2009, they were written for the thousands of readers in more than 140 countries who receive *Ethics Newsline®*, our free web-based news publication, each week from the Institute for Global Ethics.

From some angles, the narrative arc of this financial collapse appears to be one of deep, duplicitous corruption. From other angles, it looks simply like a tale of gross executive in-attention. In the current crisis, however, such distinctions may not matter. We've learned something, tragically, from the case of the text-messaging Los Angeles train driver who on September 12, 2008, took his mind off his task and killed 25 passengers: Unwitting inattention can be just as deadly as deliberate corruption — and just as unethical.

But this is also a book about hope. In the three decades since I began writing weekly columns, I've been committed to solution-oriented journalism. What most interests me today is how we get out of this crisis. Regulation will help. So will a more balanced media, willing to point out successes, positive developments, and pathways forward even while it describes the wreckage in sometimes harrowing detail. But in the end, the only genuine corrective lies in creating broad-based, authentic cultures of integrity within our organizations and institutions. This book, I hope, begins to steer us toward that conclusion.

And I do mean *begins*. This book is not a conclusive analysis, nor does it pretend to be a comprehensive history of the period. But I hope it's more than a mere scattering of observations. In assembling these pieces, I've been struck by the way that each week's news kept building the case for an ethics recession. Perhaps that's not surprising: Journalism is always the first draft of history. I've also been struck by the heartfelt *cri de coeur* that has been rising around this topic. As I was preparing this book, I kept noticing how many voices from across the political spectrum were speaking out in search of an ethical framework for our times. In a single week in mid-December 2008, for example:

- Former Hewlett-Packard chair and CEO Carly Fiorina wrote that "at no time in human history have we been so unconstrained by our array of capabilities or so challenged by our worst excesses. Never have common sense, good judgment and ethics mattered more." (*Wall Street Journal,* December 12, 2008)
- Pulitzer Prize-winning economist and *New York Times* contributor Thomas Friedman opined that "the Madoff affair is the cherry on top of a national breakdown in financial propriety, regulations and common sense. Which is why we don't just need a financial bailout; we need an ethical bailout. We need to re-establish the core

balance between our markets, ethics and regulations."
(*New York Times*, December 17, 2008)

- President-elect Barack Obama, announcing his nominee for head of the U.S. Securities and Exchange Commission, noted that "there needs to be a shift in ethics on Wall Street. . . . We can have the best regulators in the world. But everybody from CEOs to shareholders to investors are going to have to be asking themselves not only is this profitable, not only whether this will boost my bonus, but is it right?" (Press conference, Chicago, Illinois, December 18, 2008)

If, as I'm coming to suspect, future historians look back on our era as the beginning of the Integrity Revolution — following on logically from the Industrial Revolution and, more recently, the Knowledge Revolution — such comments may provide useful evidence. And if President Barack Obama read the public mood correctly when, in his January 20 inaugural address, he called for "a new era of responsibility," that revolution will happen willingly, peaceably, and deliberately.

In seeking to put this particular first draft of history into a coherent order, I've occasionally changed a column's original title, modified a phrase, or replaced a term like "last week" with a date. I have not, however, sought to update my perspective on the week's news with later information, preferring to let the columns stand as a reflection of the moment in which they were crafted. I've also arranged these columns into three sections, adhering chronologically to their dates of publication only when necessary:

- **Section 1, "The Ethics Recession,"** focuses sharply on the financial crisis itself — where it came from, how we can understand it, and how we get out of it. Making the point that the public conversation now has moved irreversibly from finance to integrity, it reflects on how we are redefining ethics away from mere *compliance* and into *values,* on the sudden jolt that has shifted moral progress from an *evolutionary* to a *revolutionary* process, and on the need to respond to the crisis not simply by creating *more ethical leaders* but by building *more ethical cultures* within organizations.

- **Section 2, "Ten Challenges,"** identifies some specific mental constructs that impede our ethical progress: short-termism, a compliance mentality, endemic corruption, uncontrolled technology, lack of political will, black-and-white polarizations, deliberate anonymity, workplace intimidation, a tolerance for the high costs of low integrity, and lousy decision making. Until we get a handle on each of these challenges, we will not have addressed the fundamentals that drove us headlong into the ethics recession.

- **Section 3, "Why Integrity Matters,"** offers some reflections on what makes us care about ethics in the first place. It starts with a reading of the falling moral barometer. It continues with a brace of columns on two central questions for our age, one of which is metaphysical ("Is ethics futile?") and the other practical ("Why is the news so negative?"). The seven columns that follow seek to provide positive answers to those questions by sharing examples — some as large as

Hurricane Katrina, others as small as a Maine garage —
that elevate integrity, expand openness, and contemplate the possibility of perfection.

This book would not have been possible without the
persistent and tireless efforts, week in and week out, of Carl
Hausman and Jeff Spaulding, the editor and managing editor,
respectively, of *Ethics Newsline.* In addition, my hat is off in a
deep and sweeping bow to Polly Jones, whose advice and effort
made it possible to pull these pages together rapidly and
accurately; to Andrea Curtis, who worked energetically with us
on the design; to Graham Phaup, executive director of the
Institute for his strong and consistent support; and to the
Institute's board of directors and staff for providing wise counsel and creative insights as these pieces were written and the
book assembled. Finally, I owe unbounded thanks to my wife,
Elizabeth, for her years of unflagging support and her ability to
grasp the concept of ethics from the inside, articulate its
importance in matters large and small, and understand the
transformative importance of these ideas for the broader world.

Rushworth M. Kidder
Rockland, Maine
February 1, 2009

Section I

The Ethics Recession

"The emergence of new theories is generally preceded by a period of pronounced professional insecurity . . . generated by the persistent failure of the puzzles of normal science to come out as they should. Failure of existing rules is the prelude to a search for new ones."

—Thomas Kuhn, *The Structure of Scientific Revolutions*

Chapter 1

It's the Culture, Stupid!

E nough hand-wringing. It's time for a solution-oriented approach to the current economic crisis. To get there, we need to ask three questions.

First, what caused it? We may never fully know. Some probable causes are easy to understand, like Wall Street excesses, regulatory inattention, and unscrupulous mortgage lending. Others are nearly incomprehensible, like derivatives, collateralized debt obligations, and credit default swaps. Still others are too amorphous for words — ghostly fears that leap like pale sparks from market to market, spooking investors and scorching trust.

But running like an obbligato beneath them all is the persistent murmur of a single word: *unethical*. There's a feeling in the air that what's happened has been not simply illegal but profoundly immoral. There's a sense that core decencies have been demolished, integrity dissolved, and common values trampled upon to an unprecedented degree.

Second, who's to blame? Not just the leaders. There's a

growing recognition that entire organizations, not just their top executives, can go off the rails. Like individuals, corporations can develop wholesale cultures of greed, fraud, and deceit. Regulatory agencies and congressional committees, too, can slide into irresponsibility, blame shifting, and turf wars. Sure, we take grim satisfaction in seeing top executives nailed for turpitude. But our intuitions tell us that the problem is bigger than that. In some organizations, the culture itself is so toxic that few employees dare call attention to misconduct — and is so deaf that whenever anyone does speak up, nobody listens.

Third, what can be done? In the coming months, the media will gorge on scandalous tales of malfeasance, as CNN already is doing in a listing titled, "Ten Most Wanted: Culprits of the Collapse." Useful? Sure, if the fault lies in individuals. But if we're going to shift from suspicions to solutions, we need to look not just at personalities but at organizational cultures. We need to know not just what makes bad ones worse, but what makes good ones better. We need, in other words, the "Ten Most Wanted" characteristics of cultures of integrity — what they are, what they do, and how to build them.

So here's a start. Based on years of research at our Institute, we think cultures of integrity arise when organizations do the following:

1. **Embed ethics in every action, strategy, and policy.** Walking the talk, such organizations bring their stated cultures into alignment with their practiced cultures — and spread that alignment from the custodian right up to the board chair.

2. **Define ethics not simply as right versus wrong but as**

right versus right. Moving past black-and-white rigidities, obvious iniquities, and I'm-right-you're-wrong oversimplifications, they learn how to make nuanced ethical choices when both sides have powerful moral arguments.

3. **Engage moral reasoning to shape future decisions.** Not content simply to use core values to explain past actions or current circumstances, they develop early warning systems to address over-the-horizon ethical dilemmas before they arise.

4. **Focus on intrinsic rather than instrumental values.** They know that the latter (diligence, say, or competitiveness) are as important to the mafia as to themselves. So they ground themselves in *really* big values, like truth, respect, and fairness.

5. **Emphasize moral principle over legal compliance.** Recognizing that lawfulness is vital, they also know the dangers of the mantra, "If it ain't illegal, it must be ethical." Legal principle is playing by enforceable rules; moral principle is obedience to the unenforceable.

6. **Expand their moral perimeter.** Some people have great honesty or responsibility, but practice these values only within their own firm, family, or tribe. Cultures of integrity constantly expand the inclusiveness of their ethical concern to embrace the global.

7. **Focus on relationship building, not just deal making.** Knowing that truly important relations are not transactional but values-based, cultures of integrity have multiple bottom lines that measure not just financial but social, environmental, and ethical success.

8. **Cherish and repeat fireside stories.** Cultures of integrity point with pride to their own moral traditions, educating new employees through narratives about taking courageous stands, making character-building decisions, and putting principles above personalities.

9. **Maintain deep reserves of moral courage.** Though prepared to take stands for conscience, cultures of integrity don't need to expend those reserves internally — while in unethical organizations, good people need huge courage just to get through a workday.

10. **Keep the ethics flame alive collectively.** Since *culture* means "how *we* — not *I* — do things around here," cultures of integrity make ethics the responsibility not of an exceptional individual's probity but of an entire community's sense of honor.

If every organization in the world approximated these characteristics enough to warrant the "culture of integrity" label, we'd be left with only one question: How could a financial crisis like the one we're in ever happen again? If we want the answer to be, *It couldn't*, we need to solve today's problems in ways that ensure such crises never recur. How? By deliberately building cultures of integrity across business and government. Nobody said that's easy. But nothing less will do.

October 20, 2008

Chapter 2

Ethics and Chocolate

It's said that people buy more chocolate during economic downturns. Maybe it's the only fun they can afford. Maybe it's a cheap pick-me-up, or an escape mechanism, or a longing for simple childhood comforts. Whatever the reason, chocolate apparently is countercyclical: As the economy slows, chocolate sales rise.

I'm beginning to suspect that ethics also is countercyclical. Over the years, I've sensed a deepening of public concern over moral issues whenever the economy falters.

If that's so, the news from mid-June should not only benefit Hershey's and Cadbury; it also should drive ethics higher up the national agenda. With stocks sliding, oil prices rising, the housing market dragging, Midwest crops flooding, and global food shortages appearing, we well may see a greater interest in returning to ethical basics.

But why? Is there a link between moral insolvency and an economic slowdown? That suspicion has now been renewed with the arrests of two former executives at Bear Stearns (which was bailed out by the feds in March in a high-profile effort to stabilize the housing market) on charges of fraud related to the credit debacle. Canadian investigators have also brought criminal charges against three former top executives of Nortel, the Toronto-based telecommunications company long revered as a safe investment, in connection with an accounting scandal that severely rattled Canadian markets in 2004.

There also may be a link between political ethics and the economy. The Gallup Organization has released data from its May 2008 survey showing that Republicans are particularly concerned about "the overall state of moral values." This year and last, 51 percent of Republicans felt the nation's moral condition was "poor" — up from a steady 36 percent between 2002 and 2006. Views of Democrats and independents, however, still sit at the 36-percent level.

The result puzzled Gallup's analysts, who could find no apparent reason for this partisan anomaly. But surely there are a few options:

1. **Quagmire**. Gallup asked participants about 16 issues, including abortion, homosexuality, cloning, gambling, polygamy, and divorce. Unlike their liberal colleagues, conservatives may feel stalemated on many of these fronts, leading to pent-up frustration that finally surfaced in this poll.

2. **Skew**. Gallup's list didn't include national security, education, immigration, or other current issues fraught with ethical overtones. Those issues might have given Republicans more reasons to applaud.

3. **Definition**. Listing only topics in the news, Gallup effectively defined morality in public-policy terms. Had Gallup used a virtues-based lens — asking about values such as honesty, respect, responsibility, fairness, or compassion — would Republicans have expressed less concern?

4. **Exhaustion**. President Bush's approval ratings are in the cellar, even among some conservatives. With little time left to address ethics issues — and little visible appetite in the administration for doing so — once-loyal Republicans may be throwing in the towel.

But suppose Gallup got it right. Suppose a newly energized slice of the nation is, countercyclically, sounding the moral Klaxon. Have they recognized that unethical executives who deliberately wreck their companies may inadvertently be destroying whole economies as well? Are they sensing that while economic downturns can stem from broad, global forces, this one may have been abetted, at least in part, by local chicanery and turpitude? Are they realizing that a politics of divisiveness, animosity, and stalemate is not only inefficient and negligent but fundamentally immoral? Are they recognizing that when times are good, nobody wants to rock the boat with this "ethics stuff" — but that when times are tough, we face hard questions from the helmsman of our conscience? Are they feeling that perhaps we've overdosed on global resources — and that the globe finally may be pushing back?

If ethics is increasingly in demand, what the seekers will most need aren't platitudes and surveys but ethical pathways and decision-making frameworks — structures to help embed integrity and resolve moral dilemmas all the way from the kindergarten couch to the CEO suite. But they'll also need to be assured of something else: This didn't need to happen. We didn't have to wait for an economic shock to wake us up. We're not so dumb that we can't contemplate and correct our ethical future before it catches us unawares. And we're not so hedonistic that we happily trash the moral long term as long as the short term feels great.

How do we know we're not? Because, apparently, when times get tough we still care enough to be morally counter-cyclical.

June 23, 2008

Chapter 3

"Hey, I Got Structured Products!"

B efore the economy soured last year, a friend of mine got a call from his stockbroker, who was recommending a new kind of "structured investment product." Trying to explain it, the broker gamely began reading from the information in front of him. But the more he read, the more muddled he got.

Finally, my friend asked him some simple questions: What comprised it, how long it lasted, how it really worked.

"I could just see him scratching his head," my friend chuckled. And finally the broker said, "Look, I'll send you the whole thing, and you can read it yourself!"

My friend is himself an accomplished portfolio manager — and this was his chosen broker. Yet here were these two professionals, trying to make sense of a product that, as my friend says, was described "in language that probably even lawyers couldn't understand."

The product? It was a derivative made up of bundled subprime mortgage loans — exactly the kind of vehicle that has

11

tanked in recent months and sent the economy into a dive.

That dive may persist, though in congressional testimony last week neither Treasury secretary Henry Paulson nor Federal Reserve chairman Ben Bernanke was predicting a recession. But whatever we call it, the financial downturn raises profound moral questions. Was it caused by blameless human error? A failure of complex computer technologies? An infestation of unforeseeable software bugs? Or is there an ethics component here? Are we seeing not cyclical collapse but cynical collusion? Is this a loss of market value — or of moral integrity?

For answers, I turned to Marshall Acuff, who in 31 years with Smith Barney became its managing director and remains a widely quoted media guru on markets and investments. In his view, the driving force of the current downturn was the increasingly speculative nature of the housing market.

"People just wanted to get involved," he said, "and they didn't pay adequate attention to the hows and the whys and the whats." Nor did the banks, eager to write loans, pay much attention to the credit-worthiness of borrowers or their ability to repay. When borrowers defaulted, the bubble began to burst.

But would the bursting, on its own, have generated the current situation? Not, he feels, without the investment banks. In an effort to extract even more profitability, they began bundling thousands of individual subprime loans together and selling them as securities.

"One could be somewhat cynical," Acuff notes with his characteristically Southern diplomacy, "and say that the new products were not fashioned in a manner in which someone without a great deal of technical knowledge" could understand them.

To put it more bluntly, as New York attorney general Andrew Cuomo's office is fond of doing, the question is whether the investment banks deliberately withheld information about the significant risks inherent in these products. He's investigating that question and may bring charges if laws have been violated.

But what if these products skate just inside the law? Even if these products were *legal*, were they *ethical*? Did they honor such core moral values as truthfulness, respect, and responsibility?

Truthfulness, it would seem, requires full disclosure of risk and an honest desire for clarification, which Acuff finds missing here. Instead, he sees some similarities to the collapse of Enron, whose managers put together arcane, complex financial instruments to "create the impression of growth when in fact there isn't that much growth."

Respect for the client also has suffered, as sellers of these products took advantage of a certain giddiness in the temperament of the times. This sort of deception, says Acuff, "typically happens when times are good" — again, as in the Enron period. Selling such products is harder, he says, when times are "more challenging" and people are being more careful and "going back to the basics. But when times are good — "'Hey, I got structured products!'"

But in the end, the issue comes down to responsibility. "The banks themselves, and perhaps even the government, should have some responsibility for educating the public," he says. Policymakers also should move strongly to restore equilibrium, which he feels is happening, and they should impose "stiffer requirements" to make these products understandable. He also faults the credit rating agencies — Standard & Poor's, Moody's, Fitch Ratings — for giving such high marks to these products.

But the real responsibility, he feels, lies with the individual. "If something isn't simple enough that you can understand it in two minutes," he says, "I'm not sure you want to get involved with it."

"At the end of the day, you can have all the regulation out there," he says, "but if someone doesn't take responsibility to become educated, then the risk of this sort of thing probably will continue to exist. You should know yourself, you should know and understand what it is that you want to do and how you want to do it."

Knowing yourself is, essentially, a question of values. In markets, as in life itself, you can't substitute rules for values. Yes, new products need regulation, but there's an enormous moral hazard in pretending that public law can relieve us of personal responsibility. In the end, the marketplace is more mental — and moral — than we like to recognize.

February 18, 2008

Chapter 4

Fannie, Freddie, and the Little Gray Lies

A dmittedly, it's a complex story. July's plunge in the market values of Fannie Mae and Freddie Mac, the two institutions guaranteeing home mortgages in the United States, now will be used as evidence for any number of arguments. Should there be tighter regulation of the mortgage business? Were the rating agencies largely to blame? Were there too many dangerous innovations such as collateralized debt obligations? Would lobbying reforms have prevented the favored treatment granted these quasi-governmental giants? Most important, should Congress now use public funds to save Fannie and Freddie, or are these two behemoths, as London's *Financial Times* opined recently, nothing but "socialist turkeys coming home to roost in the U.S., home of free-market capitalism"?

Good questions, all, and worthy of expert debate. But unless we also see this debacle as a fundamentally ethical issue, we won't extract its most useful lessons. Simply put, what brought Fannie and Freddie to their knees were millions of little gray lies. These petty fudgings misstated potential home-owners' levels of income and overlooked un-creditworthy histories. They happened over a decade. They occurred during conversations between potential borrowers and some mort-gage lenders. They were often well meaning, sometimes noble, and invariably part of a bullish trend. And while, like lone locusts in a plague, no single lie was particularly significant, taken together they darkened the entire financial sky.

Like locusts, too, these exaggerations aren't very com-plicated beasts. In fact, their simplicity made them look in-nocuous, for three reasons:

- *They seemed morally acceptable.* Home ownership, after all, long has been touted as an unmitigated good. The more homeowners, the better, especially in a rising market where a home is the largest asset for most families. To deny a family access to this investment vehicle seemed unfair, elitist, almost unpatriotic. Wasn't there, in fact, a moral imperative for banks to engage in com-munity lending rather than to practice old-style "red-lining" of neighborhoods and denial of credit to deserving people?

- *They seemed financially reasonable.* What if some lenders accepted their customers' self-reported income levels at face value without confirmation? Wasn't that a form of trust? What if, in conversation, lenders en-couraged buyers to embellish what they reported they could earn in the coming months, thereby qualifying themselves for larger loans? Wasn't that smart financial counsel? Who could fault lenders for explaining that inflation probably would raise their clients' incomes in the future, while mortgage payments would hold steady? And who could deny that buyers were invariably grateful to learn they could afford to borrow more than they thought?

- *They seemed so inconsequential.* Yes, these little lies would lead some families to slide into bankruptcy. But if most others did not, each default would be balanced by scores of well-performing loans. Wasn't that, after all, the same model used so successfully by high-end venture capitalists and down-market credit-card vendors? Hadn't they learned to thrive by taking risks and counting on a certain number of failures as the price of success?

In other words, the little gray lies all seemed so reasonable — except that they hinged on a high tolerance for deception. Which is why, at bottom, regulation alone won't set the mortgage market right. Unless the ethical mindset changes — unless lenders impose strict self-discipline on those in their fraternity who tolerate this pettifogging — the regulations will be either so incremental as to invite clever weaseling or so draconian as to stifle economic activity. And unless borrowers recognize that lying has real consequences, they won't easily be regulated into higher ethical standards.

This won't be easy. As a culture, we've long winked at little white lies on the grounds that they're victimless crimes, isolated and harmless. But Fannie and Freddie may force us to rethink our winking. They remind us that when little white lies grow gray and concentrated, they turn black as a cloud of locusts, making us all victims as they devour everything in their path.

July 14, 2008

Chapter 5

Does Corruption Really Matter?

That first week of August they fell like dominos, three in a row:

- On Monday, a German court convicted a former manager at Siemens, Reinhard Siekaczek, of operating slush funds within that massive electronics and engineering firm to pay bribes around the world.
- On Tuesday, Alaskan senator Ted Stevens, the most senior U.S. Senate Republican in history, was indicted for filing false financial disclosures that hid an estimated $250,000 he received from an Alaska-based company that included a remodeling of his vacation home.
- On Wednesday, Ehud Olmert announced that he would resign as prime minister of Israel amid suspicions that he took bribes from a Long Island philanthropist and collected multiple reimbursements for individual airline flights.

Two of these three must be presumed innocent unless courts find otherwise. So the issue is not so much with the people as with the common theme of corruption. Alaska alone, in fact, could provide enough corruption cases to round out the rest of this column. So could Siemens, which is expected to file charges this week against its former CEO and its former chairman — two of some 300 current and former employees under suspicion in a bribery scheme worth an estimated $2 billion. In Mr. Olmert's case, the tentacles may spread well beyond Israel, with serious ramifications for the Middle East peace process.

So the real question is not, Who's the latest bad guy? If that were all, *Ethics Newsline* could simply become a police blotter, tut-tutting each week over global miscreants. Nor is the question, How big is global corruption? Estimates from the World Bank put it at trillions of dollars annually. Nor is it even, How important is it? An ongoing poll on our website ranks corruption at the top of nine tough challenges facing our global future.

No, the real question is, So what? Corruption is so big, pervasive, and timeless that it's tempting to shrug it off as messy, inevitable, and intractable. Or even brazen: When lawmakers in Juneau recently came under fire for corruption, some of them reportedly donned "C.B.C." baseball caps, standing for "Corrupt Bastards Club."

So I was intrigued when, in a conference call last week with some U.S. school superintendents, the "So what?" question arose. They're seeking to bring ethics into the classroom — since, as one said, "every kid who leaves school is going to be faced with ethical decisions." But they're up against skepticism. They need persuasive arguments to prove that ethics matters

— using examples, they said, drawn from politics, current e-vents, and cases like Enron.

That's why last week's news was so useful. Siekaczek, Stevens, and Olmert remind us that corruption involves the hubris and selfishness of power. It requires subterfuge and lack of transparency. It poisons the atmosphere of trust, making cynics of the citizenry. It rides roughshod over honest competitors in business or politics who refuse to bribe. It creates the illusion of a decently refereed playing field while biasing every call. In other words, it attacks the moral roots of free, fair, and open democracies, rendering them exclusive, deceitful, and opaque.

Corruption, then, may be the most insidious challenge on the planet. Samuel Johnson once defined courage as "the greatest of all virtues; because, unless a man has that virtue, he has no security for preserving any other." Perhaps Johnson would agree also that corruption is the greatest of all anti-virtues, because unless our leaders avoid it, they have no security in resolving our toughest global threats. For Siekaczek, Stevens, and Olmert to lose their careers would be unfortunate, but for the world to suffer a void of moral leadership in global engineering, governance, and diplomacy would be devastating — a terrible price to pay in return for what, in the end, may be no more than a few contracts in Munich, airfares in Israel, or home repairs in Alaska.

August 4, 2008

Chapter 6

Ethics in a Time of Crisis

Crisis invites introspection. As the markets tumble, credit freezes, and pundits mutter about the end of free-market economics, individuals and nations are revisiting their principles. What they're finding is an age-old truth: At times of momentous challenge, there's a tremendous yearning for straight-up integrity and sound ethical analysis.

That's different from political or economic analysis. The former helps explain last week's hesitation waltz, as members of Congress weighed the electoral costs of voting for the financial rescue plan. The latter helps us understand the symbiosis between Wall Street and Main Street, and why only demagogues think we can cut the former adrift without sinking the latter. These two kinds of analysis provide the default languages of journalism — the way reporters typically write about the world. These days, however, neither language brings us to the crux of the matter, which is essentially ethical. We've finally got to confront the question of whether the way we run the world is not simply politically astute or economically feasible, but whether it's right.

Fortunately, we have a clearer understanding of "right" than we had two decades ago, when the seeds of today's financial problems were sown. In 1987 it still was fashionable to assert that ethics was relative, situational, negotiable, and wholly subjective. That year, too, the movie *Wall Street* gave us Gordon Gekko, the Ivan Boesky-inspired character with the signature line, "Greed is good." In the years since, there's been a curious divergence of paths. On one hand, philosophy and public thought — and parts of the corporate world — increaseingly have rejected moral relativism, recognizing instead that humanity shares a core of ethical values centered on honesty and responsibility. On the other hand, the financial community — or at least some parts of it — have drifted along on Gekko's surf, clinging to a moral relativism that dismisses ethics as the "soft stuff" that impedes serious progress.

The question is, Which parts of that community? Before we can cleanse the current mess, we need to distinguish innocent human error from gross moral turpitude. Did this crisis arise because well-meaning people — CEOs, regulators, congressional committee members, traders, investors — simply took their eyes off the ball as the system grew more complex? Or was the crisis caused by fraud, deceit, and corruption — by mortgage lenders coaxing unwary buyers into unconscionable debt, banks fudging their figures, and lobbyists growing rich by misrepresenting Fannie Mae and Freddie Mac? If it was the latter, individuals need to be convicted and reparations paid. If it was the former, the system needs to be restructured and new regulations designed.

I suspect history will show us that it was some of both. For starters, then, there are two obvious courses of action:

- **Build better regulations**. If greed is the demon, we need up-to-date, applicable restraints. It's been said that some of the new financial instruments are so mathematically complex that only a handful of people in the world actually understand them. Regulation always has sought to prevent the marketing of the inexplicable to the unwary. Perhaps it now should require financial institutions to demonstrate an elegant and ethical simplicity in their product lines.
- **Create better enforcement**. Under the market deregulation of recent years, the hope was that self-regulation — always the best form of enforcement — would work. Predictably, however, a financial community still mired in ethical relativism was never really going to embrace self-enforcement. Hence the need for new structures of punishment — and a diligent, well-paid, mature cadre of enforcers who can demand tough penalties that won't be shrugged off as simply a cost of doing business.

But none of this will matter unless the regulations also require that, within our financial organizations, we take vigorous steps to create genuine cultures of integrity. Unless we can build into the corporate DNA a commitment to honesty, responsibility, respect, fairness, and compassion — in other words, to doing what's right — all the regulation and enforcement in the world will create only more high-stakes efforts to game the system. Creating such cultures of integrity won't be easy: The Ethics Resource Center found in 2007 that only 9 percent of U.S. companies had strong ethical cultures. But the need increasingly is recognized: The Revised Federal Sentencing Guidelines provide favorable treatment for companies that "promote an organizational culture that encourages ethical conduct and a commitment to compliance with the law."

If there's a silver lining to the current crisis, it's that public demand seems to be building for a culture-of-integrity movement. If this crisis grew out of greed and corruption, such a movement is obviously the right response. But it's also the right response if the crisis arose from well-meaning leaders who weren't paying attention. Sadly, we now have evidence — from a text-messaging commuter-train engineer in Los Angles who accidentally killed 25 people in September — that well-meaning inattention isn't good enough. In financial markets, too, we can define such a thing as culpable indifference — and trust that even indifference can be remedied under a strong culture of responsibility.

Bottom line? We'll emerge from this crisis with a stronger commitment to integrity, a chastened revulsion against ethical relativism, and a firmer grasp on right. We didn't need a crisis to get us there. Now that it's here, however, there's a growing clarity that the way out lies along the road to ethics.

October 6, 2008

Chapter 7

This Insubstantial Pageant

W here does wealth go when it evaporates? That question might have sounded merely academic ten days ago. No longer. In this brief period, the current economic crisis has morphed into something new.

In early October, the crisis was discussed largely in the language of numbers and trends. The conversation was carried on by an earnest coterie of financial experts, with the public looking on.

Now, at the end of October, it's increasingly a conversation about values and identity. It's being carried on in the public square by individuals from all walks of life, with experts looking on and wondering how to contribute.

The earlier conversation asked what was happening, how the downturn would affect us, and when it was going to change. Today's conversation is more likely to ask who we are, why we believe what we do, and what's right. The discourse is shifting from money to metaphysics, from finance to philosophy, from economics to ethics.

That much is clear from looking at two archetypal appearances last week. The first was a two-page news-paper ad from the John Templeton Foundation in the *New York Times* on Sunday, October 19. (Full disclosure: The Institute for Global Ethics has received grants for work on character education from the John Templeton Foundation.) The ad featured essays by thirteen distinguished scholars and public figures from various political and economic perspectives, ranging from former world chess champion Garry Kasparov and French philosopher Bernard-Henri Lévy to former Pennsylvania senator Rick Santorum and former Labor secretary Robert B. Reich. The question they addressed was, "Does the free market corrode moral character?"

Even without reading the essays, you can see that this ad stands as a telling artifact of our age. *Get serious about big moral issues,* it seems to proclaim. *The question of the hour is not just about economics. It's about the potential for markets to corrupt integrity.* Had this ad appeared three months ago, I suspect it would have been met politely but dismissively. Instead, it suddenly is asking the questions on everyone's lips: Has capitalism failed? Has trust been shattered? Is our financial culture in moral default?

The second archetypal appearance last week — by former Federal Reserve chairman Alan Greenspan, speaking to the House Committee on Oversight and Government Reform — was equally stunning. Although focused on economics, the conversation broadened into the philosophical and personal when Greenspan admitted that he was "shocked" to realize that his free-market ideology had been proved wrong.

"I made a mistake," he told the October 23 hearing, "in presuming that the self-interests of organizations … were best capable of protecting their own shareholders and their equity in the firms." He noted, too, that the "whole intellectual edifice" of risk management had "collapsed" in the summer of 2007. Translated into lay language, Greenspan's mistake lay in believing that players in financial markets, left to their own devices, would self-regulate simply because it would be profitable to do so. Instead, self-regulation failed — and wealth simply evaporated.

But where did it go? Shakespeare raised a similar question about drama: Where do plays go when the curtain falls? In *The Tempest*, Prospero, the one-time duke of Milan, finishes watching a play-within-the-play and announces that "our revels now are ended." The actors themselves, he notes, have "melted into air, into thin air." The stage-set they once inhabited — "The cloud-capp'd towers, the gorgeous palaces, / The solemn temples, the great globe itself" — shall, he says, "dissolve" and "leave not rack behind." Summing up all that's left, he describes it as "the baseless fabric of this vision" and "this insubstantial pageant faded."

What's become of the wealth that seemed on paper to be so great? Is it, like Prospero's revels, little more than the "baseless fabric" of a vision we mistook for reality? Has this last decade been but an "insubstantial pageant" that, once full of gorgeous glitter, has now faded? And if it has left "not a rack behind," where did it all go — and can it come back?

These are not unanswerable questions. But they'll only be resolved by addressing the big philosophical issues that finally have broken through into public thought. If free enter-prise corrodes moral character, how can we construct a cor-rosion-proof culture of integrity? And if what Greenspan called the "whole intellectual edifice" of modern financial instruments is, in the Bard's words, "baseless" and "insubstantial," how do we rebuild it on a responsible, fair, and honest footing?

These questions are about ethics, not economics. At last we're giving them heed.

October 27, 2008

The Third Language

It's been said that if you wanted to define *water*, you wouldn't ask the fishes. In a similar way, the last people capable of defining the current financial atmosphere may be the news junkies. So immersed are they in their craft — its headlines, news flashes, commentaries, and backstories — that they rarely remember that news is *framed* rather than *ordained* They forget, in other words, that they're seeing the world through a particular mind-set, language, or paradigm.

That latter word belongs to Thomas Kuhn, whose 1962 classic, *The Structure of Scientific Revolutions,* introduced the idea of a paradigm shift. More on Kuhn in a moment. To understand paradigms, however, just scan the headlines. What you'll find is that nearly everything we know about the financial crisis has come through one of two languages, that of economics or that of politics. The first examines wealth, studies numbers, and asks, "Where's the bottom line?" The second looks at power, tracks influence, and asks, "Who's winning?" These two ways of coming to terms with the world have become the default languages of journalism.

31

The problem is that today's situation — a global economic crisis shot through with political interventions — is rapidly outstripping the capacity of these frames to explain it. As a result, a third language is coming into play — the language of ethics. Talking not about wealth or power, it talks about values. Tracking neither numbers nor influence, it examines moral sensibilities. Instead of asking about bottom lines or winners, it asks, "What's right?"

Under the influence of this third language, what began as a discussion of money has shifted into a conversation about metaphysics, character, and integrity. This shift came clearly into view during the third week of October, bookended by the twin iconic figures of investment guru Warren Buffett and former Federal Reserve chairman Alan Greenspan. On October 17, Mr. Buffett proclaimed his intention to buy and hold stocks regardless of uncertainties in the market. His op-ed piece in the *New York Times* was a powerful declaration, looking back over a long personal history of successful investing. Framed in the language of economics, it seemed to make sense of a familiar world.

Six days later, Mr. Greenspan told a congressional committee that, having trusted overmuch in the markets' capacity for self-regulation, he was in a state of "shocked disbelief." In a public recalibration of his long-standing free-market principles, his testimony pushed through into an introspective examination of identity. While still relying on economic and political framing, it had more than a hint of a moral discourse as it accepted the presence of a new world around us.

Can things really change that fast? Here's where Kuhn helps. As a historian of science, he was intent on explaining how revolutions in scientific theory come about as we move from, say, Copernicus to Newton to Einstein. Though he's writing about science, his thesis helps explain how wholesale changes in thought typically happen:

- They arise, Kuhn writes, after "frequent and deep debates" over methods and standards, leading to "the need constantly to reexamine ... first principles" — as Mr. Greenspan was doing.
- They are "generally preceded by a period of pronounced professional insecurity," arising from "the persistent failure of the puzzles of normal science to come out as they should" — showing up today as a lack of confidence in economics itself.
- They grow from a sense that something is "fundamentally wrong" with current ways of thinking, especially in the presence of a "cumulative acquisition of unanticipated novelties" that scientific researchers (or Treasury officials) can't explain.
- Political revolutions, like those in science, arise when a minority of the community senses that "existing institutions have ceased adequately to meet the problems posed by an environment that they have in part created."
- Significant change, whether political or scientific, is less evolutionary than revolutionary, less gradual than sudden, and often encounters significant resistance from the community's most respected members — some of whom are in Congress.
- While such change is sometimes anticipated, usually "no such structure is consciously seen in advance."

Instead, "the new paradigm, or a sufficient hint to permit later articulation, emerges all at once, sometimes in the middle of the night."

True, there are significant differences between scientific and economic change. But what if the analogy works? What if today's economic mistakes can't be corrected within the system? What if this "persistent failure" indicates that our "first principles" are "fundamentally wrong"? What if this turmoil presages an entirely new order of thought, where ethics is integral to free enterprise rather than simply an adjunct to it?

I'm not arguing for an ethics revolution. I don't think economic and political language will join alchemy and the four humors in the museum of outgrown paradigms. But public thought is clamoring for philosophical depth and personal integrity, articulated in a language where right counts as much as wealth or power. If that clamor leads to a more ethical capitalism and a more moral democracy, don't be surprised if the change emerges all at once in the middle of the night

November 24, 2008

Chapter 9

A Trio of Miscreants

If there were a *Guinness Book of Ethics Records*, the second week of December, 2008 would surely be in it. Over a five-day period, in tragedies almost operatic in scale, three outsized personalities crashed to the ground through their own scheming.

Most notable was Illinois governor Rod Blagojevich, arrested December 9 on federal charges of conspiring to solicit bribes in the filling of the U.S. Senate seat left vacant by Barack Obama's election.

Two days earlier, a respected and high-flying New York attorney, Marc Dreier, was picked up by federal authorities for stealing $113 million — just since October — by selling worthless promissory notes appearing to come from the firms of some of his own clients.

Then, on December 12, one of Wall Street's legendary traders, Bernard Madoff, was arrested at dawn by federal agents and accused of running what may be history's largest Ponzi scheme, defrauding his clients of perhaps $50 billion.

Fraud, sadly enough, is a daily affair, so three cases in a week isn't unusual. What distinguished last week was the gall and scope of the perpetrations. Gov. Blagojevich wasn't just selling drivers' licenses, as his (now imprisoned) predecessor, Gov. George Ryan, had done. He allegedly was marketing one of the nation's highest offices to the highest bidder.

Nor was Mr. Dreier just scamming a few innocents. He reportedly was deceiving sophisticated investors, in part by tricking receptionists into letting him bring his potential customers into the conference rooms of the very firms whose letterhead he used to create the phony loan documents.

And Mr. Madoff wasn't guilty of making just a few bad trades. At $50 billion, he is accused of collecting and losing half again as much as the entire Detroit auto industry requested earlier this month from a government bailout.

The grim symbolism here is that this trio of miscreants represents the three institutions — politics, business, and the law — that lie at the heart of our nation's current financial crisis. Given democracy's checks and balances, we typically can survive corruption in one institution if the others are sound: Bad politicians are done in by good laws and honest financing, and corporate corruption can't endure government oversight rooted in legal integrity. What was so jarring was the triple whammy — the sense that all three sectors are now vulnerable. Is there no place where the standard of ethics remains inviolable? Is there no safe moral haven left?

No, not unless we build it. There's no infallible metric we can use to measure self-aggrandizement, hypocrisy, and deception. Our only security lies in creating an ethical culture — not just better individual politicians and bankers and lawyers, but a climate that makes it easier and more natural for governors to act responsibly, financiers to take pride in honesty, and lawyers to love fairness.

Is that hopelessly idealistic? Not if you look back over the lifetime of Western democracy. In two centuries, we've managed to create an astonishing standard: a broadly shared expectation that most people will do the right thing. In part that's because we've evolved one of the fairest and most inclusive judicial systems in history. But it's also because, as democracy and free enterprise developed in the nineteenth and twentieth centuries, it was always understood that they required a moral basis, a set of shared principles to guide each participant. For some people, those principles grew out of religion or a spiritual sense. For others, they flowed from a sense of honor, community, pride, and self-respect.

What last week tested so forcefully may be the core question of our time: Can democracy and free enterprise survive without deliberate, conscious attention to their moral compasses? If those principles decay — or, worse still, go untaught and undefended — must these institutions collapse? What happens to our legal profession when people graced with the finest educations — a Marc Dreier, say, with degrees from Harvard and Yale — apparently feel no moral tether? What becomes of the political culture when elected officials have no ethical filter to separate what they *can* do from what they *ought to* do? What transpires in finance when a forty-year reputation for probity turns out to have been based on fraud and deception?

Thirty years ago, America's public schools were locked into so-called values-neutral education, where teaching ethics was discouraged. Last week reminds us how well our institutions reflect our teaching: When you cultivate values-neutral mindsets, you get values-neutral leaders. We don't have to wait thirty years to undo the oxymoron of values-neutral democracy, free enterprise, and law; it appears they will undo themselves. But we can't wait a moment longer to begin creating the cultures of integrity that may prevent December's opera from being serialized.

December 15, 2008

Chapter 10

Fighting Ponzi with Ponzi?

H e sat on charitable boards and gave to university endowments. His company was sought out by investors and touted in business circles. True, there had been suspicions, but an investigation by the U.S. Securities and Exchange Commission (SEC) several years ago came to nothing. But last fall after federal agents got wind of fraudulent activities through an insider confession, his firm collapsed in what authorities called a giant Ponzi scheme. He's now been indicted and remains under arrest for a scam that ran un-detected for more than a decade and lost billions of dollars from hedge funds, nonprofits, religious organizations, and individuals.

It's the story of Bernie Madoff, the disgraced New York investment broker arrested last month, right? Well, yes and no. In fact, the paragraph above exactly describes a situation that surfaced several months earlier in Minnesota. It concerned a high-flying Twin Cities entrepreneur named Tom Petters, who claimed to be selling electronic goods to big-box stores, using phony invoices to get loans and attract investors. In a scary parallel to the Madoff story, Petters was arrested in October after one of his top executives turned herself in to federal authorities and began secretly recording the conversations that led to his indictment.

What's scary about the parallel is that, compared to Madoff's $50 billion loss, Petters' $3.5 billion loss invites us to use the word *mere* to describe it — so jaded have we become in the current atmosphere of massive scandals, bailouts, and stimulus packages. What's scary is that we never seem to learn, from scam to scam, that they all have one thing in common: con artists who exploit the human lust for beating the system and getting rich quick. What's scary is that these swindlers come in so many flavors — slick and charismatic, like Petters, as well as aloof and mysterious, like Madoff — that they're hard to spot.

What's scary is that federal regulators in each case did not know what was happening — and still wouldn't had high-level insiders not blown the whistle. What's scary is that while Ponzi schemes aren't new (taking their name from Charles Ponzi, who ran a notorious pyramid scheme in Boston that collapsed in 1920), they are now so leveraged by new technologies that Ponzi himself couldn't have imagined their speed, scale, and reach. And what's scary is that if scams like these can range all the way from Wall Street bankers to Main Street retailers, how many other scams are still out there, unexposed and unchecked?

Fortunately, we're taking steps as a nation to address these issues. On the legal side, the SEC, understaffed and a-shamed, is tightening its processes, as are other regulatory agencies. And despite our complaints about the superficiality of the news media, we still encourage and reward the kind of serious investigative journalism that the *Boston Post* used in 1920 to blow the lid off Ponzi's original scheme and call in the cops.

On the ethics side, too, we're understanding more about the moral courage required when insiders who suspect wrong-doing decide to come forward, and we're beginning to make that process easier. We're developing ways to distinguish mere values chatter from real values-based action, aware that Petters' public recitation of his company's business values (innovation, agility, execution, humility, and caring) notably lacked the ethical values of honesty, responsibility, respect, and fairness that, if lived, might have kept him out of trouble.

What's more, we're increasingly sensitized to the need to build ethics into the entire fabric of our culture. In a single week in mid-December, for example:

- Former Hewlett-Packard CEO Carly Fiorina, writing in the *Wall Street Journal* on December 12, noted that "never have common sense, good judgment, and ethics mattered more."
- Tom Friedman, in his December 17 *New York Times* column, opined that "we don't just need a financial bail-out; we need an ethical bailout. We need to re-establish the core balance between our markets, ethics, and regulations."
- The next day, president-elect Barack Obama, at a press conference announcing his nominee for head of the SEC, noted that "there needs to be a shift in ethics on Wall Street" and that "everybody from CEOs to share-

holders to investors are going to have to be asking themselves not only *is this profitable*, not only *whether this will boost my bonus,* but *is it right?"*

That's all good news. But beneath it the scariest question still lurks: Are we at risk of becoming a nation of Ponzis? Are we building today's bailouts and stimulus packages to guarantee a working economy tomorrow — or are we, like Ponzi, paying current dividends out of our children's capital? Are we renewing our physical infrastructure to facilitate stronger economic activity in the future — or are we, like Ponzi, taxing new investors to pay for old excesses? Are we capable of building a self-sustaining, steady-state economy — or are we, like Ponzi, shackled to a requirement for constant growth as the only way to keep our system afloat?

In a world so hammered by broken trust, what we most need is the moral radar that distinguishes the honest broker from the con. Among our most useful tools may be a caveat of inexplicable wealth — an instinct, intuition, or hunch that sends up warning signals whenever things look too good to be true, and a willingness to act on that caveat no matter how dazzling the promises. There may be no quick fixes — not from brokers, not from politicians, not from regulators — but just quiet, steady rethinking, realigning, and reinvesting. In the end, we can't fight Ponzi with Ponzi.

January 5, 2009

Section II

Ten Challenges

"If you look at all of these [global] issues and ask what's common to them all, it's *lousy decision making.*"

—Ted Gordon, interview with the author, May 21, 2008

Chapter 11

Markets and Morality:
The Case against the Short-Term

If memory serves, my earliest acquaintance with a grandfather clock was in a bank lobby. As my mother did business with a teller behind a high marble counter, I stared around down at knee-level, listening to the stately tick-tocking of the clock's massive pendulum. It was the sound of confidence. *We're here to safeguard your money,* it said, *and nothing will break our rhythm.* Grave and perpetual, it bespoke the essence of financial order.

But suppose you stood that clock in the back of a pickup and drove it pell-mell down a potholed logging road. Imagine the pendulum, slamming randomly from side to side in the pitching truck. Not only would it be useless at keeping time; it would be lucky to survive without smashing through the polished cabinet. Violent and haphazard, it would be the epitome of disarray.

Watching the markets at the end of March, there was little doubt which pendulum symbolizes our age. As the first quarter of 2008 closed, the swings were extreme. Writing in the *New York Times* at the end of March, Floyd Norris noted that U.S. markets posted twelve sessions that quarter in which stocks either rose or fell by more than 2 percent – "something that didn't happen even once in 2004 or 2005." But the biggest change — a 4.2 percent rise in the Standard & Poor's index of 500 stocks on March 18, as the Federal Reserve cut interest rates — was modest compared to volatility in France and Germany, which bounced around in ranges above 6 percent. In Hong Kong, the Hang Seng index rose 10.7 percent on one day and dropped 8.7 percent on another, with India and China showing extreme volatility as well.

Is there an ethical issue underlying these excessive swings? I think there is, and I think it traces back to a financial short-termism that seriously imperils the free enterprise system. This trend — the quest for immediate profit at the expense of long-term financial security — is not new. In 1936, British economist John Maynard Keynes contemplated measures to "make the purchase of an investment permanent" as a way to "force the investor to direct his mind to the long-term prospects and to those only."

Recent critiques of short-termism have erupted on all sides of the political spectrum, with observers as different as Warren Buffett and Al Gore calling for change. *The Economist* contemplating Wall Street's woes, pegged short-termism as a root cause. "Spurred by pay that was geared to short-term gains," its editors wrote in the March 19 issue, "bankers and fund managers stand accused of pocketing bonuses with no thought for the longer-term consequences of what they were doing."

What's wrong with short-termism? That question underlies two studies by reputable organizations in 2006, well before the current crisis. In a report titled "Breaking the Short-Term Cycle," the CFA Institute Centre for Financial Market Integrity and the Business Roundtable Institute for Corporate Ethics called for reform of "practices involving earnings guidance, compensation, and communications to investors." It declared that companies need to "make adjustments to their involvement in the 'earnings guidance game'" — the practice of providing quarterly assessments of earnings prospects to Wall Street analysts, thereby encouraging investors to look only at immediate, bottom-line results rather than Keynes's "long-term prospects." It also called for executive compensation to be based on "long-term strategic and value-creation goals" rather than on these quarterly targets.

That same year a Conference Board report, "Revisiting Stock Market Short-Termism," spoke presciently about today's situation. "The pressure to meet short-term quarterly earnings numbers," it asserted, "can cause undue market volatility." Such whipsawing, in turn, can "cause management to lose sight of its strategic business model," compromise global competitiveness, and fail to invest in "such critical long-term focused areas as research and development and environmental controls."

These reports set forth the financial case against short-termism. But what about the ethical case? In themselves, neither short-term nor long-term thinking is "wrong." In fact, situations that pit our present needs against our future obligations are so common that we use the phrase *short-term versus long-term* as a paradigm to describe some of humanity's toughest right-versus-right dilemmas. And for good reason. All of us must honor the short term by spending for today's necessities. To say, "I won't eat today — I can do that next month," is not an option. But neither can we say, "It's boring to bring in the harvest — let's just live for the moment." There's a moral case for both the long-term and the short-term — and frequently a need to choose between them.

But as with the other decision paradigms we use in our work at the Institute for Global Ethics — individual versus community, justice versus mercy, truth versus loyalty — an excessive focus on one side over the other invites unethical behavior. In successful decision making, the two are kept roughly in balance. When one side continually drowns out the other, volatility rules and moral chaos ensues.

That's nowhere truer than in short-term-versus-long-term dilemmas. More than the other paradigms, this one helps explain why market volatility is an ethical issue. Think of short-termism as consumption and long-term thinking as investment. Then remember that the issue driving the recent downturn — the housing market — represents something that, for most Americans, is the largest and most long-term investment they will ever make. Yet consumption — cashing in on rising markets to make immediate profits — represents one of the fastest ways to make money that most Americans have ever seen.

Does it now make sense that whatever would seek to destroy investment for the sake of consumption could be considered unethical? True, there are lots of financial causes for today's downturn. But unless we recognize that behind them all lies the twenty-first century's addiction to excessive short-termism, we'll never address the ethical cause. Instead, we'll just keep driving down that potholed road to nowhere — and wondering what all the clanging is about.

March 31, 2008

Chapter 12

Compliance Versus Ethics:
Lessons from a French Fraud

O kay, naptime's over. That persistent crashing noise we heard during the autumn of 2007 — the sound of mortgage-lender portfolios caving into rubble — should have roused us. But only in January 2008, when a hurricane-force fraud blew the roof off French bank Société Générale, did we finally wake up.

What we're now seeing, as we rub our eyes, is a truth as vast as it is unfamiliar: that capitalism can't survive in the absence of integrity.

If that seems an overstatement, let me explain. For decades, ethics has been viewed in much of the business community as a soft topic. Some business schools, to be sure, have instituted small but lively ethics programs. And many strategists would agree that if you can manage to fit ethics into your corporate framework, you'll reap pleasant honors and appreciative comments. But competitive capitalism is still largely understood to require something other than the core values of honesty, fairness, responsibility, and respect.

As a result, the fallacy has grown up in some circles that moral values are irrelevant. Why? *Because we have all these regulations.* Get the rules right (the argument goes), enforce them vigorously, set up risk-control offices to assess the dangers and enforce obedience, and you won't need ethics. All you'll need is compliance.

The result of that fallacy is now painfully clear: a $7.2 billion loss for Société Générale, based on trades initiated by a 31-year-old employee named Jérôme Kerviel. Because Kerviel had worked for several years in the bank's risk-control area, he easily evaded the regulations. Even as late as November 2007, when Eurex, the derivatives exchange unit of Deutsche Börse, raised questions with Société Générale about some of Kerviel's trading positions, he produced fake paperwork to cover his tracks.

According to the bank's initial assessments, Kerviel was a rogue trader working alone — hacking into computers, borrowing other employees' computer passwords, and falsifying documents. By the time he was discovered, he had placed bets in the marketplace worth $73.5 billion — more than the bank's market worth. He appears not to have profited personally from his trades, nor to have wanted to harm Société Générale. His goal, according to the Paris prosecutor in the case, was to enhance his reputation and become a star trader.

There's a lot we don't yet know about the Kerviel case — whether the bank turned a blind eye to his deceptions because of his prior successes, whether others at his level were doing similar things, whether he was a scapegoat to turn attention away from the bank's mounting losses in the subprime market. But even in its early stages, his case raises serious questions about the limits of risk control:

- The derivatives market in which Kerviel worked is a specialized arena depending on complex mathematical formulas and sophisticated computer technologies. It became part of the bank's business in 1987 — and is unlike anything that earlier generations of traders had experienced. As Kerviel proved, the scale and technological refinement of this business allowed the unethical activities of a single individual to be amplified rapidly into a world-class calamity. Given the ability of technology to leverage ethics in this way, how complex will risk-control operations need to become — and will they end up costing more to maintain than the trades are worth?

- While such ethical leveraging is not new, Kerviel set a record. Société Générale's $7.2 billion loss far outweighs the damage done by Joseph Jett at Kidder Peabody in 1994 ($350 million), Nick Leeson at Barings Bank in 1995 ($1.4 billion), and Yasuo Hamanaka at Sumitumo in 1996 ($1.3 billion). This trend suggests that many lessons remain unlearned by risk managers — and that a lot of illicit skills can readily be acquired by today's young traders. Is risk control largely a palliative, building a false sense of confidence while cloaking the deeper issues underlying such rogue events?

- If Kerviel's motive was partly to prove he could outsmart the system, he may be a bellwether for a new generation of computer-genius rogues whose reward is less financial than psychic. And if, as many suspect, the subsequent termination of billions of dollars of his trades by Société Générale caused an already unstable market to slide toward wholesale meltdown, did he ultimately get the largest psychic buzz of all — seeing his own work steer the U. S. Federal Reserve Bank toward a historic rate cut? If this is what a single trader, motivated neither by greed nor revenge, can do in 2008, what might a malicious group of traders do in the next decade to sabotage an organization, a market, or even a nation?

Don't misunderstand: Risk-control mechanisms are crucial and must be strengthened. But to imagine that today's challenges can be addressed simply by better controls and tighter compliance is sheer fantasy. Which brings us back to the relationship of capitalism and ethics. The best protection any corporation can put in place is not a regime of compliance but a culture of integrity.

What if, at Société Générale, there had been a determined insistence on honesty, responsibility, fairness, and respect — not just as theories and mottos, but as practiced and admired values? What if ethics had been continuously taught, discussed, and promoted across the firm? What if an expectation of integrity had permeated the organization from the top down, reaching into every client relationship, every promotion decision, every new hire? Would rogue traders make it very far up the chain before being found out? Would even the aroma of sleaze at the desk next door have been tolerated — or would someone have had the courage early on to take Kerviel aside and point out that "we don't do things like that around here"? Would Kerviel himself, feeling the pressure of a values-driven culture, either have steered himself into honest behaviors or decided to leave?

Trust, after all, is what sound capitalism always has relied on. Last week's wake-up call reminds us that trust arises not just from a smart system of rules but from a genuine culture of integrity. If half of the effort Société Générale spent building internal controls had gone into creating a world-class culture of ethical values, does anyone really think it would be where it is today?

January 28, 2008

Chapter 13

Dujiangyan's Unnatural Disaster

Those who think ethics is merely an option — one of life's electives, rather than an essential for survival — need to look closely at a photograph from last week's news. It shows a pile of post-earthquake rubble in China's Sichuan Province. Taken by a *New York Times* photographer, it captures all that is left of Xinjian Primary School, once a four-story building in the city of Dujiangyan. According to the accompanying story, several hundred children died in its May 12 collapse.

What makes the photograph remarkable, however, is not the rubble. It's the two buildings flanking the pile. One is a kindergarten some 20 feet away. The other, a ten-story hotel, stands behind the site. Neither was seriously damaged. Nor was the Beijie Primary School, a five-minute walk away. Beijie, however, is for the children of the elite. Xinjian was for poorer children.

Last week, parents whose children died at Xinjian rose

up in anger at government officials. They suspect something went terribly wrong not just in the delayed relief efforts but in the school's original design and construction. They point to poor-quality steel and to concrete weakened by too much sand and too little cement. As one of them told the *Times*, "This is not a natural disaster."

Are these parents right? Yes, in the sense that while violent geological events are "natural", they only become disasters through human failure. These failures sometimes are charged to specific areas of study — engineering, architecture, hydrology, economics — or to related technological and logistical arenas, like transportation, emergency response, or building inspection services. But the real problem lies in the human application of ideas and practices within these areas. Hundreds more children could well be alive today if over time these applications had been managed rightly.

So what went wrong? In a word, ethics. It would appear that whenever nature breeds wholesale disaster, ethics already has failed to some extent among those in charge. It's probably safe to say that before a single floor collapsed at Xinjian or a single pillar buckled, there already had been an ethical collapse, a buckling of integrity. These moral failures are most visible in three ways:

- **Negligence.** In its tamest and subtlest form, moral failure begins with well-meaning managers and officials who are so beleaguered and overwhelmed that they neglect their obligations. When the tyranny of the immediate pushes the potentially devastating into the background, the polite phrase is *deferred maintenance.* In reality, what's happening is the slow, impersonal, hardly visible assembly of a time bomb. The Xinjian Primary School apparently had a history of problems: Some years earlier one wing had been declared unsafe, torn down, and rebuilt. In hindsight, those in charge should have allocated more funds to reconstruction — and demanded results. If ethics is about fairness, neglecting Xinjian while building higher-quality schools nearby is profoundly unethical.

- **Incompetence.** If the negligent knew they were inviting disaster, they still might be vigilant. Incompetence, by contrast, is more dangerous, simply because those in charge usually know they lack the requisite knowledge and skill yet push forward anyway. Globally, a lot is known about designing safe schools in earthquake-prone areas and establishing standards for their construction. If laborers are hired despite not knowing how to implement those standards, that's an ir-responsible tolerance of incompetence — especially if the laborers are only there because they're someone's relative, neighbor, or loyal lackey. Find wholesale in-competence and you'll also find the lack of another core ethical value, responsibility.

- **Corruption.** Neither negligence nor incompetence is necessarily unlawful, and each can be corrected by knowledge. Corruption, by contrast, is the worst kind of unethical behavior. It wallows in illegality, recognizes its own evil, and has no desire for correction. It can destroy even the most dutiful and competent organ-izations. Bribery, shakedowns, graft, and other pocket-lining ploys of the powerful — these unethical behave-iors, according to the World Bank, cost the global economy more than $1 trillion annually. The parents in Dujiangyan had every reason to be suspicious that someone, somewhere, was paid off to build a sub-standard school — a towering dishonesty that no one could call ethical.

Negligence, incompetence, and corruption, then, sit along a rising scale of unethical action. But they have one thing in common: Each can kill widely and indiscriminately. Consider the roots of death and destruction in the Chinese earthquake — and in the Indonesian tsunami in 2004, Hurricane Katrina in 2005, and the Myanmar cyclone in early May. Then consider the still-fashionable canard that ethics is merely an option, having no important place among the toughest issues of global governance, economics, or security. That anyone in the twenty-first century could hold both of those considerations simultaneously and still be considered wise is simply bizarre.

June 2, 2008

Chapter 14

Gremlin Ethics: The Moral Control of Technology

O ver the weekend my assistant emailed me to say she'd just spoken with a client. "He will be in a meeting from 4 to 5 P.M. today," she wrote me, "but asked if you could call him on his cell phone, and he'll step out of the meeting to talk."

Good client, pressing message — so you reach for the phone, right? Except that it seemed a little odd. He and I had worked closely together last spring, but we hadn't been in touch for several months. So why the urgency? Yet my assistant is a trusted source. So why doubt her message's veracity?

As her email arrived, I was sitting down to write this column about a major e-mess: the Google-facilitated debacle that caused United Airlines stock to shed more than $1 billion in market value in 12 minutes on September 8, 2008. The mess arose when a six-year-old news story about United's pending bankruptcy mysteriously resurfaced — and was mistakenly re-published as current news. Maybe that's why, instead of picking up the phone, I checked the date on my assistant's email. It was nearly six months old. That's when I remembered I'd seen it before.

Who knows how, in the netherworld inside our computer servers, the gremlins conspire to disguise six-month-old emails as new messages? Had I made the call, my friend would have been perplexed and I embarrassed. But at least no-body would have been out a billion dollars. And that's the point: The gremlins we tolerate on the personal level become intolerable in the global arena.

In United's case, the chain of events is clear — up to a point. On Sunday, September 7, a Google Web crawler, auto-matically trolling for interesting stories, found the notice of United's bankruptcy in 2002 on a current Web page of the *South Florida Sun-Sentinel.* The crawler made the story accessible to an employee at Income Securities Advisors, a Florida investment advisory firm, who then posted the headline electronically on his company's wire service.

That posting made the story available to the trading terminals at Bloomberg News, the widely followed financial news and data company. That exposure in turn triggered auto-matic sell orders by computers programmed to react within seconds to breaking news. That selling trend was noticed by other computers, and the race for the bottom began. It ended only when United spotted the sell-off and refuted the rumor.

Could this juggernaut have been stopped? Google and the Tribune Company, whose *Chicago Tribune* published the 2002 United story and which owns the *Sun-Sentinel,* have been trading blame and doing further investigations. And what a-bout the employee at the advisory service? Had he read further into the story, he would have recognized it as old news. But he didn't read further since time was of the essence: The faster his clients (or their computers) got the news, the quicker they could react. Even if he hadn't posted it, someone else might have.

What remains unclear — and oddly undiscussed — is how the story ever got from a six-year-old archive to the day's current news. Was it the same gremlin that sent my six-month-old email, or did a human put it there? If it was a gremlin, this is a story about our inability to exercise ethical and responsible control over the technologies we invent — and perhaps our *unwillingness* to do so, lest we impede the headlong pace of life in the financial lane. All that was needed was the intervention of human judgment. But judgment slows you down — even if only for a minute or two, as editors confer in a newsroom about a story, a headline, or a placement. Yet judgment is why readers still turn to news organizations, rather than just mucking about on the Web for themselves. What does it tell us if, at a news organization as sophisticated as the Tribune Company, no human backstop was in place to keep old stories off new pages?

On the other hand, what does it tell us if they *did* have a backstop? Could an unethical individual, holding such a position at some newspaper, conspire to launch such a story? A person, say, who loves to create havoc? A computer geek proving he can manipulate the world? A disgruntled former employee getting back at some company by targeting its stock? A savvy investor who buys when the shares hit bottom and sells when they regain their value? A terrorist seeking to wreck a market and bring down a nation?

In a world where computers now read our papers, assess our probabilities, and trigger our sales and purchases, the moral control of technology has never been more important. It's long been true that technology leverages our ethics, megaphoning minor turpitudes into major calamities. It's now clear that gremlins can create as much calamity as humans. And since we can't teach ethics to gremlins, our only choice is to root out the gremlins with the same moral determination we bring to cracking down on hackers or disabling terrorists. We can't afford to dismiss the cause of the United stock blip as just another glitch. When technology is this important in our lives, being pretty good isn't enough. Either we control our technology, or it controls us.

September 15, 2008

Chapter 15

Freeman Dyson's Gasoline Tree

L ate last week, as the price of a barrel of oil surged $11 in a single day, I recalled a conversation I had in the fall of 1986 with one of America's leading scientific thinkers, Freeman Dyson. The 1979 oil crisis was still a sobering memory, but Dyson, a theoretical physicist at the Institute for Advanced Study in Princeton who described himself as "obsessed with the future," wasn't worried about energy.

"I don't regard that as a real problem," he told me during an interview for *The Christian Science Monitor*. "If you have advanced biotechnology, I don't see any difficulty in getting all the energy you want from the sun. It's only a question of redesigning trees so that they produce something other than wood — gasoline, for example."

This was before the age of email, laptops, cell phones, or the cloning of Dolly, the Scottish ewe. So does that mean, I asked somewhat incredulously, that we'd get fuel the way we get sap from a sugar maple in New England — by tapping the tree?

"I wouldn't do it so crudely," he explained. "I would have a sort of living, underground pipeline system, so that the gasoline would be delivered where you want it."

For a man who designed a nuclear-powered starship and long had been a proponent of space colonization, energy sufficiency was simply a matter of inventiveness. But how far into the future would it be? "At the most," he said, "50 years."

We're now about halfway there, and Dyson's prophecies — about which he continues to write — no longer seem so strange. Last month on PBS, "NewsHour" reported briefly on Solazyme, a California high-tech startup that has reengineered the genetic structure of algae. Processed in laboratories for a few days, it produces oil very similar to the light sweet crude that nature requires tens of millions of years to create. Solazyme already is running several cars on its product.

Why can't I buy some for my car? Because, obviously, the innovation is still under way. But that's no excuse for other alternative-energy resources. Here on the Maine coast, the wind is typically steady and strong, and we have more sunny days than Michigan or the Pacific Northwest. But I have no windmill in the yard, no solar panels on the roof.

Now you can blame me for not being a tech-savvy early adopter like a few of our neighbors happily living off the grid in south-facing houses with basements full of batteries. But that's not the point. Why aren't alternative-energy technologies as common as cell phones and broadband — not restricted to the clever and the forward leaning, but spread across millions who only want their benefit and couldn't care less how they work?

Because (the theory goes) the answers don't lie in the technology but in the economy. As long as oil is relatively inexpensive, there's not much demand for these new technologies. Let gas prices hit $10 a gallon (or so it is thought), and all of that will change.

But will it? If prices rise slowly, the boiled-frog syndrome may set in, with nobody thinking to leap out of the pot until it's too late. If, on the other hand, the increase is sudden and sharp, the clamor for change could cause massive disruptions in family budgets, prompt panic at the gas pumps, and raise the specter of profiteering in alternative-energy products.

In fact, we have a better choice. Rather than waiting for markets to force painful adjustments, we can create policies to speed up change. Suppose, ten years ago, Congress had legislated changes that vigorously promoted entrepreneurial solar and wind-power equipment. Suppose, as a result, my local Yellow Pages listed as many local firms selling and servicing this equipment as there are car dealers — and as many banks willing to finance it as to provide auto loans. Suppose I could realize substantial tax savings by equipping my home with equipment powered by wind or sun. Is there any doubt that, even though Dyson's genetic wonder world still may be two decades off, our little Maine community already would be well on its way to energy sufficiency?

What's holding us back? The answer has nothing to do with technology and everything to do with political will. In the end, our political progress depends on the moral choices we make and the ethical decision making we pursue. Effective national policymaking requires three things: agreement on shared values, methodologies for creating compromise when values conflict, and the moral courage to put those methodologies into practice. Around the politics of energy policy, we're seeing a few proclamations about values. But as last week's partisan muddle in the Senate over a global warming bill suggests, we're seeing far fewer efforts to hammer out the compromises that create sound post-petroleum economic policy — and hardly any moral courage in leading the march toward that goal. Will we simply wait until the economic hardship falls so harshly and unfairly on the nation's households that some of them are destroyed? Or are we ready to demand more responsible forethought from our policymakers — so that, as Dyson observed, energy continues not to be "a real problem"?

June 9, 2008

Chapter 16

Educating for Nuance

Want evidence that the global moral barometer is in steep decline? Look at Myanmar, where the ruling generals blocked outside aid from reaching cyclone victims. In the end, when history does its tally, the deaths caused by a tyrannical government working in secret may far outnumber those caused by the forces of weather.

Want evidence that the barometer is rising? Look at China, where the government responded to an earthquake by sending in thousands of soldiers and taking unusual steps to share the story with the outside world. History may eventually note that this disaster, coming so close upon the opening of the 2008 Olympics, forced a new openness in this once-secretive nation.

So which is it? Is the barometer rising or falling?

Questions like these were on the table in May when I joined a group of Nova Scotia public-school educators to consider questions of ethics. Dividing the group down the middle, I asked half the room to list as many arguments as possible —

quickly, in bullet-point form — to indicate that ethics is in free-fall and that the world is plunging deeper and deeper into turpitude. The other side had the charge of arguing the opposite — that the barometric uptick is taking us incrementally but steadily toward a more ethical future.

As you might imagine, the conversation was rich and varied. Each time the negativists tossed out a point, the upsiders came right back with a rejoinder — and vice versa. Within moments the room was thick with problems, from AIDS and cheating and global warming to Enron and pornography and Eliot Spitzer. But the countercurrent was just as strong, with talk of diversity, recycling, charitable giving, energy conservation, gender equity, and Nelson Mandela.

"So which is it?" I finally asked. "Is the barometer rising or falling?"

"Yes!" someone replied. His quip was met with a general chuckle around the room. Why? Because we all recognized the impossibility of any such oversimplification as I had proposed. It was a nice answer.

But I think the best answer is, "That's a really dumb question!" Over the years, I've had scores of similar conversations with groups in various parts of the world. People often come into these discussions with a bias toward cynicism or optimism. But when forced to confront the range of evidence — even briefly, under broad headings without detailed analysis — they quickly sense the complexity of the issues and the difficulty of making a categorical judgment. Optimists are sobered, cynics are undermined, and a quiet sense of moral nuance sets in.

These days that moral nuance is hugely valuable. At every turn, it seems, our public discourse demands that we commit ourselves to categorical judgments. Going out in public without an opinion somehow feels like arriving at the supermarket without your pants: You can function fine for a while, though sooner or later someone's sure to notice and ask you to explain yourself.

That's especially true when ethical issues are at stake. We may feel uncomfortable taking positions on topics requiring specialist knowledge — immigration, the economy, healthcare policy, future sources of energy, or the like. But on the broader topic of ethics we feel an impulse, even an obligation, to speak up. We feel the need to chart the ebb and flow of responsibility, respect, fairness, compassion, and honesty. And well we should. Ethics is first and foremost a personal topic, open to every voice and inviting each individual's response. While it sometimes can appear academic and arcane, it's actually an immediate set of ideas, grasped through intuition and reasoned out in commonplace language. Everyone deserves a place in the ethics conversation — except, perhaps, those who insist that if you haven't read the right texts and don't know the proper scholastic language, you aren't qualified to talk about this most commonplace of topics.

Yet that very commonality poses a threat to ethical discourse. It can turn too easily into unwarranted certainty, smug self-confidence, and prickly assertiveness. The startling superficialities that pass for opinions on cable television and in today's blogosphere remind us what happens when a culture of glib obduracy replaces a culture of reasoned questioning.

As we head into the election season, we may encounter a surfeit of mulish, unbending self-will on questions of values and ethics. The reaction may be to write off all moral discourse as perverse and pointless, and retreat into a disdain for any sort of ethical conversation. Needed, instead, is a capacity for moral nuance. If we remember that every claim that the moral barometer is in decline is apt to be followed by the demand, "Therefore, vote for me!" — while each claim of moral improvement invariably precedes the request to "Reelect me!" — we'll be better equipped to resist demagoguery. The more we respect moral complexity, the less we'll be in danger of falling for either the dogmatic or the dismissive. Of such quiet nuance is civil society made.

May 19, 2008

Chapter 17

Democracy Versus Anonymity:
You Can Vote, But You Can't Hide

B y the time we got there last Saturday, the annual town meeting in Lincolnville, Maine, was under way. Doris Weed shooed us in with a whispered greeting, handing us our bright teal "Registered Voter" cards without asking for identification. She's worked in the town office for decades and knows just about all of our 2,000 citizens by name.

The folding plastic chairs in the elementary school gym were pretty well filled, so we took seats down front. Up on the stage were the selectmen — they're still called that, even though two of them are women, including the chair. Joining them were the town officials. At the rostrum was Lois Lyman, a librarian and editorial consultant who had agreed somewhat reluctantly to step in at the last minute. As we sat down, she was shepherding Article 10 (of 34) toward a vote. At issue: Does the town wish to appropriate $314,417 for the municipal administration budget, or reduce that number through an amendment by trimming Karen Secotte's receptionist position back to part-time?

That, of course, was not the real question. The meeting, clearly, was still in throat-clearing mode, with the Big Issue still to come. Lois ran it with a deft hand, and under her self-deprecating grace the tenor was as thoughtful and intelligent as it was civil and polite. Which was a good thing, because by Article 12 the sparks were going to start flying. That's when we would decide whether to eliminate the entire police department budget of $110,564, effectively closing the department.

It's been said that a New England town meeting is democracy in its purest form. Everyone can speak up, everyone can vote, and every detail of the budget is available for inspection — whether it was $300 for Memorial Day flags or $80,000 to fix that dangerous intersection where Thurlow Road meets Youngtown Road as you come over the blind rise past the winery. But the past five years have been tough. Tax collections have risen 65 percent, and the trend appears to be continuing. Now, with gas prices slamming rural communities where people drive trucks to jobs that are miles from home, every penny matters. The budget committee had labored for months, agonizing over what and how to cut. The selectmen had approved their numbers and handed them over to the voters. At issue was a dilemma fundamentally moral in its structure: Will we honor the needs of the community, represented in the collective budget, or respect the needs of the individual, represented by the struggling taxpayer?

This year it came down to the police. At times we've had a local constable, and at other times we've been serviced by the Waldo County sheriff's officers. Now, with our own full-time police chief and four part-time officers, some people were happy to feel a greater sense of comfort. They worried that drug dealers already had targeted Maine's 3,478 miles of coastline — longer than California's, as it weaves around estuaries and peninsulas with more nooks and crannies than an English muffin — as a place to land boatloads of drugs unnoticed. They worried that U.S. Route 1, running through Lincolnville on its way from Canada to Florida, easily brought outsiders into the community. But others saw the police department as wasteful, outsized for a town this small, and providing a service we could have more cheaply even if it meant waiting longer for a sheriff's officer to arrive when called. They warned of a false sense of security from thinking that one patrol car could effectively cover a township of 44 square miles. And they worried in general that the town office was becoming too large and, well, too *officious*.

It had all come to head four days earlier at the June election. There, along with primary decisions about candidates for the U. S. Congress and the Senate in November, was Article 3, a referendum to "cease any operation" of the local police. It was followed by Article 4, which would amend the town charter to allow Article 3 to be implemented. While Article 3 was a classic no-means-yes question, requiring either a no vote to keep the police or a yes to disband them, Article 4 was a complex piece of legalese. Voters on Tuesday apparently had been baffled. By eight votes — 401 to 393 — they had eliminated the police, but by 17 votes they had refused to change the charter — meaning, in effect, that the police couldn't be eliminated.

Unless, of course, the town meeting refused to appropriate money. So on Saturday the forces on both sides had mustered their best arguments, with the eliminators proposing an amendment removing $110,564 from the budget. It took her a good half hour, but when Lois finally had run through the speakers on both sides and we held up our teal cards for a vote, the amendment was roundly defeated.

So Lincolnville still has its police force. But watching the process, I could see that the town has something even more important: its sense of civility, of comity, of friendliness. At the national level, democracy is being fractured and abraded by the polarizing forces of animosity, cynicism, and rant. The national media may have a role in this polarization, sparking arguments that can then be sensationalized. But Lincolnville has no national media exposure. We all live here. When we're not at a town meeting, we see each other at the post office or on the pier or down at Breezemere Park where the town band has its concerts. We can argue, but we can't hide.

Maybe that's the overlooked secret of effective democracy — that while ballots can be secret, the debate must be public. In the end, democracy and anonymity don't mix. On a national scale, and especially on blogs and talk radio, you *can* hide. You can rail and recriminate without giving your name. You can't do that in a New England town meeting. Yes, feelings can be strong, but the forces tending to keep discourse civil are even stronger.

That's why Lois needed to set an inclusive tone. That's why speaker after speaker acknowledged sympathy and understanding for the other side. What they were debating was not right versus wrong: Both sides had their share of right. That's why democracy matters.

June 16, 2008

Chapter 18

Healthcare's Deadly Bullies

T hey shout, threaten, and burst out in inexplicable rage. They won't return messages. Their language is belittling, their tone of voice condescending. They're uncooperative during routine activities and impatient with questions. But they're brilliant, successful in their fields, and key generators of revenue for their organizations.

Sadly, we all know people like that. We've even developed names for such behavior: *impolite, intimidating, threatening, disruptive, abusive,* or *just plain rude.* But chances are we stopped short of *unethical.* Why? Because however nasty and unpleasant the behavior, we're not sure it lacks moral conscience. So we write it off as a fluke of personality rather than a failure of principle. After all, we say, isn't everyone entitled to a quirk or two? And really, who is it hurting?

That last question has now been answered with surprising force by an unexpected source: the Joint Commission, the leading accrediting body for health-care organizations in the United States. Its "Sentinel Event Alert" for July 9, one of a series of brief reports on threats to health-care quality, is titled, "Behaviors that undermine a culture of safety." Summarizing years of research, it concludes that "intimidating and disruptive behaviors" in the health-care professions can "foster medical errors, contribute to poor patient satisfaction and to preventable — adverse outcomes, increase the cost of care, and cause qualified clinicians, administrators and managers to seek new positions in more professional environments."

Translated into layman's language, that means that intimidation causes mistakes, offends patients, ups costs, and drives away staff. And that's not all. Depending on how you read the quiet euphemism of "preventable adverse outcomes," it appears that intimidation, in a high-stakes medical setting, could actually kill people.

So much, then, for brushing aside intimidation as unfortunate but not unethical. It's clear that in places like Robert Mugabe's Zimbabwe, Saddam Hussein's Iraq, or Omar Hassan al-Bashir's Sudan, intimidation in the hands of tyrants ends up littering the landscape with bodies. It's also clear in school settings that unrestrained bullying, a classic form of intimidation, can be a precursor to tragedies like the 1999 shootings at Columbine High School in Colorado. Now it appears that the same impulses may have devastating effects even within otherwise well-run organizations.

On global as well as local stages, then, intimidation, which relies on fear to impose its will, is not only indefensible but unethical. But is it rare? No, says the Joint Commission study, citing research showing that "40 percent of clinicians have kept quiet or remained passive during patient care events rather than question a known intimidator." Not limited to physicians and nurses, these behaviors also "occur among other health care professionals, such as pharmacists, therapists, and support staff, as well as among administrators." Nor is intimidation restricted to gender or to certain disciplines. It is, however, somewhat foreseeable among individuals who "exhibit characteristics such as self-centeredness, immaturity, or defensiveness." What's more, the healthcare culture has "a history of tolerance and indifference to intimidating and disruptive behaviors," which "often go unreported, and therefore unaddressed" from fear of retaliation and reluctance to blow the whistle.

The Joint Commission, of course, focused on the narrow bandwidth of its own profession. But these findings reach far beyond health care. Substitute your favorite professional arena — teaching, business, law, politics, religion, government, the military — and this report still sheds a dreary light.

Fortunately, the report also includes eleven "suggested actions" for addressing intimidation. Some are strictly managerial. They include skills-based training and coaching, surveillance, interprofessional dialogue, and the use of "cultural assessment tools" to "measure whether or not attitudes change over time." But perhaps the most important message is that ethical values are essential to combating intimidation. The report's first recommendation insists that an organization's code of conduct, as well as the training surrounding it, must "emphasize respect." Peppered throughout the remaining recommendations are other core ethical values, including accountability, empathy, trust, and equity.

The report doesn't use the word *ethics*, which in healthcare circles still largely refers to medical rather than managerial issues. Yet the report's message is profoundly ethical. Intimidation may not be illegal, but it's unquestionably immoral, and the corrective lies in ethical constructs. Other professions need to follow the Joint Commission's lead. They should recognize intimidation as an issue of morality rather than manners. They should research its prevalence and destructiveness. They should insist that it be treated as a "zero tolerance" issue. And they should address it by building cultures of respect, equity, and integrity. That would put us well on our way to corralling one of society's most subtle, perverse, and destructive traits.

July 28, 2008

Chapter 19

Boeing's $40 Billion Ethics Bill

Is ethics worth $40 billion? Not officially. The stunning announcement in March, 2008 from the U.S. Air Force — that Boeing had lost a massive contract for a new fleet of refueling tankers — was couched in strictly economic terms. In announcing that the company's fifty-year franchise to build those famous gas stations in the sky had been handed to a partnership between Europe-based EADS (the European Aeronautic Defence and Space Company, makers of the Airbus) and Northrop Grumman, Air Force acquisitions chief Sue Payton insisted that the choice was based only on the "requirements of the war fighter" balanced with "the best interests of the tax-payer." It was never debated, she insisted, as a choice between jobs for U.S. or European workers. Nor was it framed in terms of the ethics of the bidders (one of which, Northrop Grumman, is, as we need to note in the interests of full disclosure, a corporate sponsor of *Ethics Newsline*).

In a year of presidential politics, with recession looming and the dollar sliding against currencies world-wide, the decision to send jobs overseas is eliciting howls of protest at Boeing's Seattle plants and in Congress. Behind all that racket, however, a quieter lesson risks being lost: the parable of Boeing as a morality play about the relationship of ethics and the bottom line.

The drama unfolds in three subplots. The first begins in the late 1990s, when Boeing employees start stealing proprietary documents from Lockheed, a competitor for government business in rocket-launching programs. In 2004, the Pentagon strips $1 billion in rocket- launch contracts from Boeing and nails the company with a twenty-month suspension of its right to re-bid — a record among major military contractors.

Meanwhile, the second subplot comes to a head in 2002, when Darleen Druyun, a procurement officer at the Pentagon working on Boeing contracts, is recruited secretly by Boeing's chief financial officer, Michael Sears, to a position within the company. In return for a promised job, she steers contracts toward Boeing. Convicted on charges stemming from this conflict of interest, both she and Sears are fired, fined, and jailed.

The third subplot erupts when Boeing CEO Philip Condit suddenly resigns in late 2003, as the above-mentioned scandals are braiding themselves together into a federal ethics investigation. His replacement, Harry Stonecipher, moves quickly to work out a settlement with the government, which by February 2005 he is predicting confidently. The settlement finally comes three months later. It frees Boeing of criminal charges relating to the earlier scandals, but imposes a $615 million fine, said to be the largest ever levied on a military contractor. But by then, Stonecipher himself is already out of office. Two months earlier, he had been sacked for having an affair with D.C.-based Boeing employee Debra Peabody, breaking ethics rules he himself imposed on the company.

Conflict of interest, stealing documents, sexual dalliances — you couldn't write a textbook case on the collapse of corporate integrity that features a more potent interweaving of unethical forces. In fact, of all of the temptations known to and studied by defense-industry ethics officers, these three are the showstoppers:

- **Procurement scandals**. When 32 major defense contractors formed the Defense Industry Initiative on Business Ethics and Conduct in 1986, it was partly in response to public outrage over press accounts of spare-parts suppliers colluding to charge the Pentagon $600 for a toilet seat and $400 for a hammer. Now the DII, as it is currently known, vigorously promotes its ethics training programs through case studies on conflict of interest. One of its training videos — involving Jim, a defense contractor, doing insider deals with Mike, an old friend who is now a government procurement officer — could have set Darleen Druyun's and Michael Sears's hair on fire by its parallels to their own situation.

- **Information theft**. An earlier case widely noted in the defense industry teaches this lesson. It began early on May 16, 1991, when William Haggett, the CEO of Bath Iron Works, a Navy shipbuilder in Maine, spent 15 minutes examining documents obtained from a competitor and then asked to have them copied. He recognized and reversed his mistake by late afternoon — and was exonerated finally by the Navy. But he lasted only three more months before his board, unable to tolerate even that 15-minute lapse of integrity, sent him packing.

- **Sexual affairs**. Of all of the pitfalls Stonecipher should have foreseen, this was perhaps the most obvious. His predecessor, Philip Condit, had fallen into that very trap by having an affair with Boeing receptionist La-verne Hawthorne. Condit had other difficulties — a penchant for lavish spending, spectacular parties, and bad financial decisions. But at least part of the reason for his firing appears to have been his tangled personal life and his fraternization with a junior employee. Now, having thought they had found in Stonecipher a well-settled grandparent and husband of fifty years, the board simply couldn't tolerate this further down-drag on the company's reputation. Ten days after they were alerted to the affair, Stonecipher, like Condit, was history.

What, then, does the public need and want from its defense contractors? Engineering excellence? Of course. Deep commitment? Certainly. But neither of these has any guarantee of surviving without ethics — a point not lost on Boeing, which diligently has been upgrading its ethics programs since Stonecipher's departure. So did these prior ethics lapses lose Boeing this contract? Better to say that a slow drip of public uneasiness with Boeing's integrity made politicians and Pentagon officials just that much more open to alternatives. It created just enough of a void for EADS and Northrop Grumman to step in and at least win a hearing.

What's the moral of this morality play? Simply this: Without an ethical wobble, there's no void. Without a void, there's no serious competition developing. Without the competition, there's no tough choice. And without a tough choice, Boeing wins. Which suddenly puts a price on ethics — $40 billion and rising — that few would have thought possible before last week. Anybody still want to argue that ethics is unrelated to the bottom line?

March 3, 2008

Chapter 20

Humanity's Worst Threat: Lousy Decision-Making

W hat is the most threatening global issue facing humanity today? Is it terrorism, where advancing nuclear and biological technologies give single individuals new opportunities to create mass destruction? Or is it violence against women, which today creates more casualties than warfare? Maybe it's CO_2 emissions, which could warm the world and melt enough polar ice to raise sea levels for 634 million coastal residents. Or is it governmental corruption, which accounts for more than $1 trillion a year in political bribes? Or perhaps it's mass migration, which by 2025 could put as many as 1.8 billion people on the move in water-scarce areas? Or is it slavery, entrapping more people now than at the highest point of the African slave trade?

To chart public priorities among these and other global issues, we did a small pilot survey of members of the Institute for Global Ethics in May, 2008. Given our mission, we wanted to know which issues raised the greatest ethical challenges to our global future.

Since the questions in our survey were based on the fifteen major issues catalogued in the 2007 "State of the Future" report from the United Nations-affiliated Millennium Project, we asked one of the report's co-authors, Theodore J. Gordon, to join us for a follow-up conference call with our survey participants. Gordon, who was a founding board member of our Institute, conceived of the Millennium Project in the 1980s and remains one of the world's most highly respected futurists. He's been studying future issues and trends since well before 1971, when he founded his own consulting firm, The Futures Group. So we were eager to share with him our results.

Of the nine topics in our survey, our respondents clustered three of them near the top: terrorism, CO_2 e-missions, and mass migration. They followed with a group of five more: corruption; violence against women; global slavery; disease, AIDS, and pandemics; and imbalanced wealth distribution. The ninth issue, shortage of medical professionals, came in well below the rest. As Gordon talked us through these results and as the respondents shared their views, I sensed they were searching for some bigger, overarching theme — some common thread that made these issues significant. I also sensed an unspoken question on everyone's mind: "Ted, what do *you* think is the Big One?"

His answer surprised us all. In effect, he said, it's none of the above. Then, in three key words, he nailed the concern we'd all been circling around. "If you look at all of these issues," he said "and ask what's common to them all, it's *lousy decision making.*"

"There used to be a time," Gordon continued, "when I

thought futures research, my field, would make its contribution by improving decision making. But I've abandoned that thought. We could have the best insight into what the future might be — through magic techniques not yet invented — and decisions would still be *terrible!*" Translation: It's not the specific issues that challenge us, but the way we fail to deal with issues of every sort.

That strikes me as a remarkable admission for a man whose life has been devoted to advancing and promoting futures research. Gordon wouldn't want me to hold him up to unfair comparisons, but if Einstein after decades of work had told us that something mattered more than physics, or if Cezanne had concluded that painting wasn't what it was all about, or if Darwin had intimated that he was outgrowing his commitment to evolution, wouldn't we pay attention?

Our leaders, Gordon emphasized, aren't bad people. But "they don't have a good grounding in decision making, because decision making is ad hoc." As a result, today's decisions often rely too much on the decision maker's reputation or on undetermined psychological factors. Worse still, decisions even can rely on what he called "creating opportunities for the family" or on "what you had for breakfast."

"Somewhere in the future," Gordon observed, "a science of decision making has to emerge." This science, he feels, must comprise such elements as futures research, econometrics, and ethics — what he describes as "a curriculum that covers the field."

Gordon's not telling us that the big, high-leverage issues on the global agenda aren't important. They matter

enormously and require every bit of energy that global organizations pour into them. They need public support, private
initiative, and collective will. But mostly they need the new,
sharp instrumentality of twenty-first-century decision making.
That instrumentality includes ethics — an ability to discern
right from wrong, coupled with a way to frame our toughest
problems as moral dilemmas that pit two right courses of
action against each other. With that in place, nothing we face —
terrorism, global warming, slavery, corruption, or the rest —
will be beyond our ability to correct.

May 27, 2008

Section III

Why Integrity Matters

"This union may never be perfect, but generation after generation has shown that it can always be perfected."

—Candidate Barack Obama in his speech on
race, Philadelphia, March 18, 2008

Chapter 21

Reading the Moral Barometer

L et's start with two questions: How would you rate the overall state of moral values today? Do you think it's getting better or worse?

Americans have little difficulty answering either question. But then, they sit in a prosperous nation, atop a long history of unrestricted religious practice, political optimism, and entrepreneurial flair. They enjoy a judicial system that pretty much works, a civil service remarkably free of bribery, and an expectation of corporate and government integrity so deep-rooted that headlines break out whenever it gets violated. In overwhelming numbers, they trust their children to the public schools, their transportation to their carmakers' engineering, and their bodies to the food sold in supermarkets and the water flowing from their taps.

So they must think America's moral barometer is high and rising, right?

Wrong. By astonishing numbers — in the four-out-of-five range — Americans say that the state of the nation's moral values is "poor" or "only fair." In telephone interviews with

1,003 adults conducted May 10-13, 2007 for the Gallup Organization's annual "Values and Beliefs" poll, only 17 percent said
that the state of moral values is good or excellent — down from
22 percent as recently as 2003. Even lower are the numbers of
those who think things are getting better: Only 11 percent see
the moral barometer as rising — less than half of the 24 percent
who said so in 2003.

Okay, now the usual objections. People complain that
these two questions oversimplify a vastly complicated topic.
They note that respondents mean different things by "moral
values." They point to a fashionable cynicism that finds the bad
in everything. They explain that some respondents think ethics
is for sissies and can't bring themselves to say anything good
about values. They worry that Gallup's results are skewed,
since their researchers only talked to people willing to talk —
and people who think things are fine have less interest in
talking to pollsters.

Even so, don't shrug off these numbers too quickly. All
those caveats also were true in 2003, before the numbers began
their slide.

It's tempting to tick off the multiple causes for this
decline — wars, doping, plagiarism, nepotism, relativism, moral cowardice, corrupt congressmen, unethical CEOs, and all the
rest. So here's a different question: What three things would
have to change — in the United States or wherever you live —
for you and those around you to say to Gallup in 2008, "It's not
quite so bad," and "It seems to be getting better"?

This question is not rhetorical, so while you're getting
out your pad and pencil, let me hazard my view on my three
things:

1. **Greater public civility**. There's a harshness to public discourse these days, an antagonism that's too quick to turn debate into confrontation and political disagreement into personal affront. Refined into edgy strategy by special interest groups screaming to be heard above the background chatter, that stridency is picked up by some in the media and parroted as the standard for modern discussion. If the tone shifted more toward respect — with dignity, listening, and that much-forgotten quality of humility more in evidence — wouldn't the public begin to sense a rising moral barometer?

2. **More personal honesty**. There's an undercurrent of deception at work in our culture. In more benign forms, it's an assumption that the truth is too hurtful, offensive, or uncertain to be shared. The more virulent form assumes that you need to lie to get ahead. While that's an old idea, it's winning new forms of encouragement and support. Cheating of all stripes, from flat-out fraud to the subtlest spin, seems to be less naturally resisted by those who in years past would have had the conviction and the courage to condemn it. If we saw more acts of honesty, greater efforts at transparency, and a more ready candor around us, wouldn't we conclude that moral consciousness was improving?

3. **Increasing evidence of fairness**. There's an injustice of exclusion in our midst these days, visible in such things as the widening income gap between the rich and the poor. There's also an injustice of neglect — showing up, for instance, in our unwillingness or inability to enforce laws concerning immigration. If democracy means

anything, it means equality of access, voice, opportunity — as well as equity of enforcement, regulation, and control. If we could see more manifestations of fairness in our daily lives — and see ourselves finding ways to express more fairness to others — wouldn't we feel a greater optimism?

But that's just my take. What's yours? If Gallup calls you next summer, how will you answer? After all, if we can arrive at a consensus on what constitutes a more moral nation, perhaps we can begin to redesign our global consciousness to get there.

June 11, 2007

Chapter 22

Is Ethics Futile?

"**D**oes ethics really make any difference?"
It was a heartfelt question. The questioner, a corporate finance executive from England, didn't strike me as cynical, ignorant, or confused. Over dinner in Vienna with his colleagues from Germany and South Africa, he was recalibrating his thinking in light of a two-hour ethics workshop earlier that day.

He'd been an active participant in that session. He liked the ideas. Working in finance, he knew the enormous value of honesty. Working internationally, he'd seen that ethics has cross-cultural validity. Working in a team atmosphere, he realized that responsibility and trust are crucial to corporate efficiency. He wanted ethics to matter. But did it?

I could see his point. Corporate executives so often get nailed in high-profile cases — corruption, fraud, sexual harassment, or whatever — only to bargain their way back to freedom and business as usual. Politicians of scant means, earning modest salaries, retire to millionaire settings. Students plagiarize, get caught, confess, and receive the faintest of reprimands.

rize, get caught, confess, and receive the faintest of reprimands. Is anyone really paying a price for unethical behavior? Is anything changing? Does anybody care?

I was thinking about my friend's concern as the news rolled in later that week. It featured two high-profile cases from the sports world in the summer of 2007 that should have given him a ray of hope:

- Floyd Landis, the 2006 Tour de France champion, was found guilty by an arbitration panel of using performance-enhancing drugs. After an extensive series of hearings, charges, and countercharges, Landis was at last stripped of his title and barred from the sport for two years. Because doping among competitive cyclers has been such an open secret — causing the sport to lose considerable cachet and some of its public base — the panel's decision was praised by (among others) Travis Tygart, the chief executive for the United States Anti-Doping Agency, who called it "a victory for clean athletes and for those who value clean and honest competition."

- Barry Bonds, the baseball slugger who in August, 2007 surpassed Hank Aaron's record for career home runs, revealed that his team, the San Francisco Giants, did not plan to renew his contract, which was paying him $15.8 million in salary. One likely reason: persistent suspicions that Bonds used steroids. The distrust has become so strong that Bonds has been booed regularly wherever the Giants travel — a distraction that to an otherwise solid team may have become insurmountable.

To be sure, each of these cases has complications. Both athletes insist on their innocence. At the time of writing, Landis had one more chance to appeal, though the expense appeared prohibitive. Bonds had not been formally charged, though his name was often mentioned in connection with steroids distributed by the former Bay Area Laboratory Co-Operative (BALCO).

Even so, these cases tell us something. Taken together, they remind us that crime still doesn't pay, that celebrities can't hide, and that even hot-shot public relations advice can't undo the weight of public opinion.

And it's the public opinion itself that most matters here. Apparently the public does care. Fans aren't shrugging off these victories. They're not inclined to applaud a win-at-all-costs attitude or tolerate a whatever-it-takes mindset. They're not buying the simplistic argument that man is no more than a cellular machine, to be redesigned and strengthened in any way possible by whatever drug comes along. They don't see steroids as progress, but as artificiality.

Why are they so clear? Because they still care about ethics, and at their core these two cases are almost perfectly unethical. Of the five core values that define an ethical mindset — fairness, responsibility, respect, honesty, and compassion — the cases of Landis and Bonds strongly call into question the first four. Using illegal substances is unfair, tilting the playing field and disadvantaging those who play by the rules. Such use is irresponsible, not only to one's own body but to fans, fellow team members, and young people who see athletes as role models. It is disrespectful to the sport itself, and especially to former stars whose re-cords get shattered by artificial means.

And it is dishonest, not only in prompting the dozens of daily deceptions required of any cover-up, but in publicly agreeing to one set of rules while privately playing by another.

Where does that leave my English questioner? No doubt (he might say) a few like Landis and Bonds do take a hit — but many don't. Agreed. But there's a larger point here. What matters is not only the number who get caught but the public desire to catch them. What we're seeing is a longing for a world of integrity. Without that longing, who boos a home-run champ? Who banishes one of the world's fastest cyclers?

Does ethics make a difference? It certainly did to those two, and to huge numbers of fans. Those fans aren't prudish puritans. They're ordinary folks who care enough about the ordinary ethical values to say, "That's not right — you don't play the game that way!" I find that encouraging.

September 24, 2007

Chapter 23

Why is the News So Negative?

―――

Here's a letter that got me thinking about negativity in the news. "I look forward to your newsletter each week," wrote Geoff Roberts, headmaster of the Crescent School in Toronto, "and on occasion have forwarded sections of it to my staff at school. What strikes me, however, is that taken on the whole, the list of stories provided are often depressing — a compendium of flawed decisions and poor leadership."

"While I find it useful to read the tales of woe and learn from others' mistakes," he continued in his September, 2007 note, "I would find it uplifting, and I think others would as well, to have a regularly occurring section in the newsletter that outlined some degree of moral courage exhibited by ordinary and extraordinary individuals. Cautionary tales have their place in literature throughout the ages, but so do inspirational tales."

Geoff need not apologize for his feelings. Remember what he'd been reading during the week he wrote me:

- U.S. attorney general Alberto Gonzales, engulfed in various ethics scandals, announced his decision to leave the Bush administration amid bipartisan criticism and loss of trust.
- Atlanta Falcons quarterback Michael Vick pleaded guilty to one criminal count of financing dog-fighting gambling operations, reversing his emphatic denials of any wrongdoing.
- Idaho's veteran Republican senator Larry Craig, after pleading guilty to disorderly conduct in a Minneapolis-St. Paul airport men's room, announced his resignation under pressure from his party's leadership.
- Congressman Rick Renzi (R-Ariz.), targeted by ethics questions and under investigation over a land deal related to his wife's business, announced that he will not seek reelection.

Meanwhile, the news was awash with stories of unethical behavior in the subprime mortgage crisis, irresponsible government and private-sector responses to victims of hurricane Katrina, and immense scams involving vendors supplying materiel for the war in Iraq. And that's just from the United States. Last week's *Ethics Newsline* also covered stories of complaints about Quebec police infiltrating protests at the North American Leaders' Summit last month and of systematic résumé fraud uncovered among leading citizens in South Korea.

Given that *Ethics Newsline* is a digest of the week's ethics news, it goes without saying that our content will mirror that of the world's news outlets. We report what we find in those sources. But does it stand to reason that those sources should be so routinely negative?

In one sense, yes. News is about what's exceptional, not what's expected. It's about the new, the different, the unforeseen. So the fact that unethical behavior still qualifies as "news" is oddly encouraging: If a wholesale lack of integrity were seen as so ordinary as to be unworthy of reporting, the news would concentrate on rare and bizarre stories of people doing strangely right things. When rightness becomes the exception, the ethics deficit is severe indeed.

But there's a more immediate question. Is the news these days more negative than five years ago, or than when we were growing up, or than it's ever been? That's tough to measure, but if we feel intuitively that it is (as Geoff clearly does), then we need to ask why. Here are three options:

1. The news really is worse, the world really is becoming more unethical, and integrity really is on the wane as never before.

2. The world's news machinery is built on fads, and the fashion of the day is to uncover hypocrisy and explode complacency. Those are laudable journalistic goals. Editors attuned to these trends will elevate them to front-page status whenever their reporters sniff them out. The downside? Given such editorial incentives, reporters may begin seeing a this-ain't-what-it-seems aspect to every story — and may find themselves deliberately or unconsciously spinning their stories to fit the pattern their editors expect.

3. We care more about integrity, and are more much more attentive to issues that we would have let slide in the past. Has no one ever before padded résumés, defrauded wartime governments, or lured the unwary with easy credit? Or do such things, which we once wrote off as sad but expected behaviors, now strike us as both exceptional and outrageous? Are we, in other words, demanding a higher standard of ourselves?

Whichever it is, Geoff is right: There's a yearning for more stories of ethical leadership and moral courage. We may not find them in the national and global news sources we cover, since heroism is often most visible at the local level. The best way for us to get these stories is for you, our readers, to alert us to them.

So if you find story candidates tucked into your local news outlets, send them to us. And if you know of powerful but unreported stories of moral courage and clarion integrity in your community, let us know. While we'll keep publishing cautionary tales, we're keen to provide the uplifting ones as well. Like you, we also need reasons to be inspired.

September 4, 2007

Chapter 24

Hurricane Katrina:
Small Virtues in the Big Easy

L ast week I spent four days in New Orleans, a city in comeback mode two-and-a-half years after the ravages of hurricane Katrina. Traveling as trustees of a charitable foundation, our group met dozens of community leaders, government appointees, business executives, bankers, demographers, environmentalists, and local residents. We saw the gray-brown watermark on the sides of buildings several yards above ground level — evidence of a flood that immersed an area seven times the size of Manhattan, in some places for as long as 56 days. We heard chilling stories of personal loss and social disorganization. Yet we also found evidence that in small but significant ways, a new political and moral order is struggling to be born — one that could shape not only New Orleans but the nation.

If that sounds overblown, consider that New Orleans is the site of one of the two great American stories of this still-young century. If 9/11 represented a major test of the nation's ability to respond to international attacks, Katrina tested our ability to respond to domestic crises. Both are ongoing stories. Both leave us wondering whether we're passing or failing. Both mark points of definitive, irreversible change.

You can't hang around New Orleans for very long without hearing people talk about change — and about the "silver lining" arising from the calamity. Environmentalists see a silver lining in the new concern for the nearby wetlands, which could have significantly reduced the storm surge if they hadn't already been degraded by decades of commercial development. Community organizers see the silver lining in the sound of once-silent citizens speaking up to save neighborhoods devastated by the floods. Economists see it in the resilience of local entrepreneurs who, working with nonprofit microcredit banks, are reopening day-care centers, driving schools, debris-removal companies, and hosts of other mom-and-pop businesses. Churches see it in once-separate black and white congregations coming together in new forms of collective action.

That doesn't mean the challenges aren't severe. New Orleans may never again reach its pre-Katrina population. Nearly 40 percent of the population, according to figures from the Brookings Institution, live below the poverty level. The destruction of 100,000 homes from wind and flood damage has wiped out family investments and pushed rents up by nearly 50 percent. The final bill for repairing present damage and investing in a new future will exceed $100 billion.

Still, the optimism is palpable. Why? Because what's also being destroyed are some old ways of thinking. The city's entrenched and infamous public corruption is at last being resolutely challenged. So is the idea that you can build houses safely without stilts — slab on grade, as they say here — on dangerously low land behind a flawed levee system. So is the idea that you can simply reconstruct school buildings in an education system ranked among the nation's worst before Katrina hit.

But there's deeper change afoot. To understand it, imagine a horizontal scale with two end points labeled, respectively, *Big government will save us* and *Big government will destroy us.* Conventional wisdom puts each of us somewhere along that scale, roughly related to our location along the conservative-liberal spectrum. So you might predict that impoverished, jobless, welfare-dependent communities in New Orleans would cluster toward the liberal end of the scale, while the city's oil-rich, high-living, internationally sophisticated communities would have little use for government.

Instead, voice after voice last week echoed that of Marylee Orr, executive director of the Louisiana Environmental Action Network. In the weeks and months following the storm, she told us, "I thought that government agencies would come forth and help us. It didn't happen." Yet there is equal skepticism, even from business leaders, about New Orleans mayor Ray Nagin's declaration that "market forces" should be allowed to determine the city's redevelopment.

In an odd way, it's as though New Orleans finds itself at right angles to that whole scale, its residents distrusting both ends points and shifting instead to live along a different, perpendicular axis. They're rolling up their sleeves and getting things done themselves, depending less on governments or markets and more on their own self-reliance. Of course they need money and regulations — two things that governments provide. And of course they need financial incentives and economic opportunities, which markets create. But in the new realism of survival, the old horizontal idolatries of either one are collapsing like shotgun houses in a storm surge.

In an election year, that collapse has ramifications for politics just as, in a period of economic uncertainty, it has financial implications. But primarily, in an age groping to understand 9/11 and Katrina, that shift has ethical consequences. In a city called the Big Easy, the easy language of bigness — in praise of big government or in adulation of vast market forces — is losing sway. Instead, in conversation after conversation, you hear the language of individual values. People here talk about responsibility for self and others. They talk about a race-blind respect for everyone's dignity. They're demanding public truth telling, a compassion for all who suffer when disaster strikes, and a justice that is incorruptible, swift, and fair.

Will that shift from horizontal to perpendicular thinking reach beyond New Orleans? Will it create a fledgling social order at right angles to the past, equally wary of governments and markets? That may depend on the nation's youngest voters — the newly energized activists who continue to pour into New Orleans, gravitate toward presidential campaigns, and distrust the politics of polarity. They, along with the people of New Orleans, may be one of the most positive stories of our time.

April 7, 2008

Chapter 25

Mike's Align

The other day I stopped by our local garage, a trim, gray-stained, three-bay affair hugging the verge of Route 1. With the Maine winter not far off, I needed Mike to put the snow tires on my car. I'd also run over a parking-lot curb one misty night the week before, so I thought I'd talk to him about an alignment.

I pulled around to the side where he keeps his 55-gallon waste oil drums, painted in different colors and lined up like a rank of pudgy toy soldiers, and recalled that I used to see Mike a lot more often. Back in the 1970s, our family owned a succession of station wagons that regularly went out of alignment. You'd touch a curb or hit a patch of potholes, and the front end would immediately develop a case of the wobbles. If you didn't visit Mike pretty regularly, you'd soon be looking at some oddly worn treads and a bill for two new tires.

But for years I hadn't thought about alignments. Why not? Maybe, despite my recent nocturnal encounter, I was driving better. Maybe there were fewer potholes — though you couldn't prove that by the road up to our house. Or maybe the cars we'd owned recently were better engineered. Whatever the reason, I couldn't recall when I last had to change tires because of those lopsided bald patches.

I went inside, and Mike and I set a time for an appointment. As I was leaving his sign caught my eye. "Mike's Align & Repair," it said, offering customers a distinction I hadn't focused on before. When something's damaged or broken, you fix it. But when something's in fine shape but a bit out of whack, you bring it back into line. Mike knows the difference between aligning and repairing, and he won't charge you for a replacement when all you need is an adjustment. That's what has earned him so many loyal customers over the years.

As I drove away, reflecting on the success of small-business integrity in rural America, I recalled a workshop we'd just conducted on moral courage. At one point, discussing the opposite of courage, we asked the participants to identify the qualities that go along with cowardice. In a few minutes we'd filled a flip-chart with words like *fearful, defensive, self-centered, indifferent, sullen, inconclusive, fretful, mean, removed, cynical, passive,* and *fractured.* Any business that merits this description will never come close to building the loyalty that Mike has. But does that mean the business is broken? Or are things simply out of line?

You hear a lot these days about the need for organizational alignment. It's not something you do in a three-bay garage, but it's a good analogy. Organizations, like cars, can get botched up. They hit economic potholes and flip off their wheel weights. They bounce hard over hidden regulatory curbs or cross ditches of morale at odd angles. And before you know it, they start to wobble. That's when they lose confidence, muffle their moral courage, and settle for a fuzzy pragmatism that borders on deceit. Mistaking bluster for integrity and stubbornness for fortitude, they slip into the moral cowardice described on our flip-chart.

When that happens, what they need is the managerial equivalent of Mike's Align & Repair. Too often, however, what they get is either Slick Willie's Fix-It-Cheap or the Royal Reconstruction Service. Though the price is different, each one's got the same answer: Things are really messed up here, so let's gut this puppy and do a total makeover.

Don't get me wrong: I'm no fan of organizational cowardice. But most of the time I suspect that what a cowardly organization needs is not repair but realignment. The thing still runs, after all: It's not as though the front wheels are at right angles to the chassis. They're just off by a few degrees. Sure, that's a key divergence, enough to keep you from running up to speed. But all it needs is someone with the right equipment and the skill to set it right.

Why? Because a lot of what seems to be cowardice isn't the opposite of courage, but the counterfeit of it. It's not that employees have set themselves deliberately at variance with moral courage. They don't hate putting integrity into practice or bringing values into action. They've just drifted off into something that looks like courage but isn't. They don't like feeling fretful and defensive, but they don't quite know where they went wrong. It won't help to tell them, "Okay, let's tear it out and start over." Nor will it do to fall back on that shallowest of excuses, "Hey, if it ain't broke, don't fix it." Those words are perfectly true in theory — and frightfully harmful in practice. Lots of things that aren't broken still need alignment.

Mike knows that. He doesn't give you a new front end, nor does he walk away saying, "Nothing's busted, so I can't help." He rolls you into the bay and tweaks your camber and toe adjustments until everything comes into line. He knows you're made of good stuff. His job is just to point all your parts in the right direction.

October 29, 2007

Chapter 26

No Empty Ballpoints

F or some years, I've suspected that by studying our pens we could learn a lot about our relationships. I know: It sounds fluky. But I think I can back up my hunch, having just conducted our first household penventory.

Don't bother looking it up — *penventory* isn't in the dictionary yet. It simply means "an inventory of all pens possessed by a single household at any given moment." I must confess, right up front, that the concept is in its early stages, without professional oversight or agreed-upon standards. I should also note that our household probably falls rather wide of the average. My wife and I do a lot of writing, so in addition to our computers we rely heavily on pens. And because we travel here and there, we've accumulated more than our share of ballpoints stamped with hotel logos — which, despite all the talk about paperless offices, are more prevalent than ever.

Still, I've done my best to carry out a competent audit. I didn't count pencils, markers, or highlighters. I excluded penless caps, refills, ink cartridges, and assorted springs, clips, and barrels. And I'm sure I overlooked pens lurking in suit jackets, old overalls, retired briefcases, shaving kits, piano benches, tool boxes, sewing chests, glove compartments, garden baskets, and (ouch) ski boots. I didn't try to categorize: For my purposes the plastic roller-ball with the pull-off cap counted just as much as the slender, gold-plated, monogrammed ballpoint with the smoothly turning twist top. Nor did I try to distinguish pens that worked from those that were clogged, hardened, jammed, or otherwise useless.

Notice I didn't say empty. My informal survey has convinced me that there are hardly any empty ballpoint pens in the universe. More on that in a moment. But first the results. Our household, as of this audit, has 159 known pens. That includes six in my nightstand and 12 in my wife's, 19 in the old olive-oil can in the kitchen, 29 in the downstairs study, and 66 in a drawer in my closet — a finding for which, as my wife knows, I have no adequate explanation.

Let's suppose, however, that she were content to use only a single, favorite pen for the next year. Let's also suppose that almost all of the rest could be scribbled, sanded, twisted, or otherwise coaxed into working, and that no new pens appeared. That would still allow me, by a quick calculation, to use a different pen each day between now and April 25, 2008.

And that, I think, is news. It's safe to assert that there has never been a society on earth, right up through my parents' generation, that could make a similar claim. My father, for most of his career as a professor, carried a fine fountain pen that he held in high regard. When I began using ballpoints in school, I got some nice ones as presents from time to time, and was crushed if they got lost, swiped, or stepped on. Only in recent decades has the pen become the one tool every student owns in greater numbers than anything else.

So naturally it's only now that our culture has any use for penventories, which serve to remind us of five sobering things:

1. We're a culture of convenience, so wedded to our ease that, if we've forgotten to bring a pen with us, we're unwilling to walk across a room to get one. Instead, we keep a couple in every drawer, assuming that they're all available for casual sharing.

2. We're a culture of obsolescence, immersed in a world of disposables where handsome-looking pens can quit working the moment we try them. Result: We expect failure, building in redundancy and hoarding backups.

3. We're a culture of hypocrisy, babbling proudly about the need for recycling while overlooking the environmental pollution arising from non-biodegradable pens. Instead, we discard them with an abandon that would appall us if applied to Styrofoam cups, printer cartridges, or flashlight batteries.

4. We're so besotted with materialism that we'd rather keep our options open than express commitment. So instead of investing in a single long-lasting pen, we use pens promiscuously, rarely expending all of the ink in any of them before losing interest and flitting to another.

5. We're woefully unobservant, crying out against convenience, obsolescence, pollution, and materialism while indulging in those very things every time we pick up a pen.

If you're beginning to suspect that a penventory is about more than just pens, you're right. It's mostly about relationships. If you doubt that, reread those five points, substituting the word *relationship* for *pen*.

That, after all, is the moral of this tale. Is the disposable relationship, in fact, the hallmark of our age? Have we been schooled to tire of long-term quality and prefer short-term variety? Do too many relationships carry someone else's logo? Are we littering the moral landscape with the landfills of half-used relationships?

As you do your own penventory, think about these things. If you top 159, let me know. I'll promise two things: I won't embarrass you by publishing your name, and I won't send the winner a prize pen.

November 19, 2007

Chapter 27

Letting Freedom Ring

L ate Saturday, as news trickled in about street protests in Myanmar, we were picking blueberries on a Maine mountainside when the phone rang.

That's a sentence I never thought I'd write. When I was growing up, berry picking meant scrambling to the tops of rocky cuts where they'd blasted the highway through the forest. It meant following no particular path, but going where the intuition took you, always searching the ankle-high bushes for the brightest and largest clusters. It meant a commitment — usually several hours — ending only when the empty Jack and Jill Peanut Butter pails were brim-full.

But mostly, it meant setting other things aside, including the rest of the world. While the word *multitasking* hadn't yet been coined, it was clear already that if you thought success meant doing several things at once, blueberrying wasn't your thing.

As the late afternoon sun raked the distant hills on Saturday, it highlighted a cell-phone tower that may have been enabling the ringing. The member of our group who answered was planning a fundraising event several thousand miles away in the Caribbean. Wandering a few feet off, she talked for five minutes with the artist designing her invitation on deadline. Then she came back to berry picking.

The nice thing about blueberrying is that it takes some concentration, but not much. It sets you loose to intersect with others and then drift apart, without need of repeated hellos or goodbyes. You talk easily when you're close by and un-apologetically fall silent when you're not.

In one of those silent periods, I found myself thinking about that ringing phone. There were phones ringing in Myanmar, too, where a ghastly and tyrannical government once again had cracked down intensely on its opponents. This time, soldiers had fired into a parade of monks and their supporters. Several were dead, and many more had been wounded.

But now, in the first week of October, 2007, something was different. Foreign journalists had largely been purged from the country, yet the news was still getting out. Armed with cell phones, video cameras, Internet blogs, and a passion for truth-telling, the public had transformed itself into a pack of amateur journalists. Never mind that the world's major news outlets couldn't get in. Never mind that the government imposed draconian censorship on local reporting. News was flowing like water down a mountainside.

And it wasn't just washing away. As the country's clique of aging despots has folded in more tightly upon itself in recent years, exiles have built news networks outside the country. Working daily with news from sources operating within Myanmar (formerly Burma), they've learned to sift fact from rumor, weigh the essential against the merely interesting, and keep their supporters informed. So when the protests broke open this past week, there were well-practiced traditions of editorial judgment. There were audiences around the world eager for the news. And there were obvious destinations for dispatches from citizen journalists.

One such destination, the Democratic Voice of Burma, operates radio and TV stations from its base in Norway. "Our station is a key factor in making a change," Khin Maung Win told Reuters last week. In 1988, a military crackdown against a massive protest killed some 3,000 people. At the time, "Burma was a completely closed country," he said, and "there was no media coverage." Now, he said, "everyone is watching."

From the perspective of a pristine Maine mountainside, it's easy to criticize cell-phone towers for spoiling the view. There's a good deal of local protest about plans to build a-nother nearby. But those protests, however they end, won't descend into bloodshed. That's how freedom works. Not only does it let technology change the way you do business, making possible new interminglings of work and leisure that were im-possible when I first went blueberrying. It also lets you pre-serve the kind of liberties Maine has and Myanmar wants.

And that's the point. What tyrants for centuries have accomplished by brute force — walling off their enemies be-hind barriers of invisibility, killing and maiming without pub-licity, viciously eliminating all reporting except what they sanction, luxuriating in a secrecy that lets them merge the grim work of oppression with their leisurely appropriation of power — is suddenly being upended. The agent of change is not tanks and troops. It's the flitting of tiny electronic impulses around the world.

Yes, there's a moral downside to the advance of cell phones. Towers litter the landscape. Kids forget how to be solitary. Students message their friends during exams to get the answers. Drivers making calls swerve off the highway. Terrorists wire phones to bombs. But there's a moral upside as well. Transparency overcomes obfuscation. Truth-telling slices through censorship. People do more in less time, with greater teamwork and fewer wasted efforts. And from Maine and Myanmar, in ways no dictatorship can squelch, freedom literally rings.

October 1, 2007

Chapter 28

Jane Austen's Globalism:
Three Lenses for the Future

———————

Oxford, England

To no one's surprise in this pre-election summer, the U.S. presidential candidates have been traveling overseas to bolster their foreign-policy credentials. Like presidents before them, their task has been, in the words of that shopworn adage, to think globally but act locally.

But what does "think globally" mean? A deceptively simple question, it surfaced during a recent meeting of internationally minded think tanks here at Oxford University. Convened by the New York-based EastWest Institute, it brought together representatives from Brazil, China, Dubai, Ethiopia, Great Britain, India, Latvia, Russia, Singapore, Switzerland, Turkey, and the United States. The stated goal was to create a world-class alliance of public-policy research organizations, provisionally called the Global Leadership Consortium. But the conceptual challenge arose from a troubling fact: Much so-called "global thinking" is little more than narrowly national thinking strutting on an international stage.

The English novelist Jane Austen, it turns out, may help us sort this out. We'll get to her in a moment. First, though, take a more homey example: U.S. energy policy. It is driven largely by national needs in the face of global pressures. True, those who think about energy — presidential candidates, for example — need to know the geopolitics of suppliers like Iraq and consumers like China. They must be internationalists, and they must travel to be so. But that's no guarantee that they will think globally. If they see their goal solely as defending U.S. energy interests, they will wear their global hats atop only a national uniform.

Genuinely global thinking, by contrast, aspires to a universal standpoint — making moral judgments, as the English philosopher Henry Sidgwick once said, from "the point of view of the universe." It seeks to rise above positions viewed by some nations as truth but by others as mere self-interest. Freeing itself from the provincial, the national, and even the regional, it gravitates toward a perception of truths so broadly acknowledged as to be apparently universal. It seeks energy policies that benefit all nations. Yes, it wears the hat of local and national action, but always as part of a global uniform.

At that notion, of course, the very walls of Oxford seem to recoil. "Nonsense!" they cry out. "How, given the multiplicity of cultures, can there be *any* universally acknowledged truths? Isn't every truth simply somebody else's fiction? How dare you disturb our exquisitely differentiated view of the universe by asserting so transcendent a commonality?"

So perhaps it was propitious that our meeting was held at Lady Margaret Hall. As the first college at Oxford University for the education of women, its walls have seen generations of thinkers demanding common educational opportunities in the face of sharp differentiations between genders. And perhaps it was not accidental that the words of Jane Austen, who never could have attended Oxford, though two of her brothers did, wafted into our conversation. "It is a truth universally acknowledged," she wrote in the famously witty opening sentence of *Pride and Prejudice,* "that a single man in possession of a good fortune must be in want of a wife."

Her words are rich with the irony of overstatement — what, after all, can a gaggle of chattering rural women be expected to know about so Oxford-like a construct as universal truth? Yet this sentence throws down a gauntlet to the naysayers. Is there a culture anywhere that disagrees with her proposition? *Shouldn't* wealthy single men get married — not for giddy romantic reasons, but for the practical social purpose of propagating children they can well afford to raise and thereby perpetuating the culture?

If we can find one such "truth universally acknowledged," might there be others? Can we, in other words, identify a basis for a kind of universal thinking that escapes the boundaries of nationalism and regionalism, looks at life from a global perspective, and sees things the way that people from a variety of cultures agree they should be seen?

In an age proud of its ability to deconstruct universals, that may seem a tall order. But one place to start looking is at ethics. It appears that some "universally acknowledged" values — honesty, responsibility, respect, fairness, and compassion —

are held in common by many cultures around the world. If that's true, global thinking can begin profitably by seeing the world through the lens of those values.

Another lens, as several of the conferees noted, focuses on trends of thought that might broadly be called expansive. Such trends move from the immediate to the long-term, from the one-dimensional to the multidimensional, from the partisan to the integrated, and from the self-centered to the community-focused. Thinkers rooted in these trends are more apt to think globally than nationally.

A third lens helps distinguish between two classes of issues. One class comprises those issues that are genuinely global — so interdependent that they lie beyond the ability of any single nation or region to control. Climate change, energy security, weapons of mass destruction, global terrorism, and the architecture of global markets all force us to think beyond the interests of even the largest nation or region — to look down from above, as it were, and see all the parts at once. A second class of issues — food security, governmental cor-ruption, low-income housing, gender equity, and education reform among them — occur across the globe but don't require that overarching view: Any single nation can make progress on them even if others don't.

Can a group of think tanks, using these three lenses of shared values, expansive trends, and interdependent issues, help promote truly global thinking? If so, they can pool their valuable national and regional perspectives to help move governments toward holistic, transnational, and universal perspectives. They can help the world's major corporations grasp the difference between the merely multinational and the genuinely global. And they can do so in ways that strengthen, rather than degrade, the local, tangible benefits that governments and businesses provide.

July 21, 2008

Chapter 29

A New President's Ethical Landscape

As Barack Obama takes the nation's helm, the greatest challenge he faces can be summed up in a single word: *ethics*.

Really? Not *economics?*

No. The nation's economic crisis already has outgrown itself. The financial recession has morphed into an ethics recession. Increasingly, as the Madoff case makes clear, the core issue is no longer money and wealth, but character and integrity.

On the surface, of course, Obama's task will be to bring together the fiscal wizards who can rekindle markets and grow assets. But the underlying challenge will be to find wizards of integrity — canny financial minds imbued with the moral authority to rebuild the nation's shattered sense of responsibility. The goal is not just to get people to *spend*. It's to get them to *trust* — a requirement for any market to function.

Fortunately, Obama's greatest resource can also be summed up as *ethics*. He comes into office on a surge of public goodwill rooted in the perception of his moral character. A

November Harris Poll found that 51 percent of voters pegged moral values as "very important in deciding which candidate to vote for." Asked what they meant by "moral values," most voters pointed to such personal characteristics as honesty and integrity, rather than to social or religious issues (like same-sex marriage or abortion) or political issues (like immigration or the Iraq war). The strength of that goodwill, evident in the crowds converging on Washington for this week's inauguration, is evident also in the numbers. The Gallup Organization's polling last week put Obama's approval rating at 78 percent, up 10 points since the November election and easily eclipsing the pre-inaugural favorables for George W. Bush (62 percent in January 2001) and Bill Clinton (66 percent in 1993).

It shouldn't surprise us, of course, that a public deeply troubled by an unprecedented ethics recession is hungering for a leader of integrity. But are his admirers endowing him with impossible attributes? Are they holding him to unattainable standards? Are they setting him up for failure?

I don't think so, largely because Obama may be one our most transparent presidents. Unlike Lyndon Johnson or Richard Nixon, there doesn't appear to be any dark undercurrent swirling below a sociable surface. Nor does he seem to have difficulties aligning reality with truth-telling (Clinton's challenge) or with ideology (Bush's problem). To be sure, Obama's transparency has been heightened by the dissection he endured under the microscope of an exhaustive campaign, but it also grows out of his very nature. Although he possesses one of the most intelligent and nuanced political minds of our era, he appears to be, paradoxically, a surprisingly uncomplicated thinker — dedicated to clarity, decidedly principled, and determinedly pragmatic.

But what about the moral landscape he's entering? Are the challenges simply too daunting, too demanding of compromise, too corrosive of integrity? Not if he and his administration grasp three things:

1. Given the public's mood, the issues he faces will need to be framed in moral terms. No solution will feel complete unless it is articulated in the language of ethics and integrity. The argument can't be phrased in the old ideological polarizations of talk radio ("I'm absolutely right, so therefore you're dead wrong and stupid to boot!"). It must be delivered in the new language of right-versus-right thinking, where each side receives a fair hearing and the dignity of civil discourse is respected.

2. Such thinking requires penetrating moral analysis of the world's toughest dilemmas. Some, like the pending question of whether Israel committed war crimes during its invasion of Gaza, will center on the age-old tension between justice and mercy. Others, like the economic bailout, will devolve into questions of short-term benefits versus long-term needs. Still others, like the war in Afghanistan, will focus on the difference between the truth on the ground and the loyalty to certain leaders, policies, or positions. Finally, a wide range of issues — healthcare among them — will pit the needs of the individual against the rights of the community. Such issues can't be addressed as black-and-

white, right-versus-wrong problems; whichever side
you're on, the other side has too much moral credibility
to be ignored or shouted down.

3. Resolving these dilemmas requires a consistent set of
   resolution principles. Under Clinton, the tendency was
   toward an ends-based, utilitarian principle, where
   ethics meant that you did the greatest good for the
   greatest number. In the Bush administration, the
   decision making was more rule-based, Kantian, and
   ideological: You invoked whatever precept you wanted
   everyone to follow, with less regard for immediate consequences. Obama well may draw on his empathetic,
   community-organizing days to invoke a care-based
   principle of reciprocity and the Golden Rule, asking
   what he would want others to do to him.

Given the ethics landscape, this is no country for moral
cowardice. The world Obama campaigned in last spring has
lost its moorings. It's searching desperately for its self-
confidence, its trust in others. It's ready for an ethics
revolution, not just an inauguration.

January 19, 2009

Obama and the Idea of Perfection

O bama the idealist. The phrase trips readily off the tongue — and for good reason. What was it that brought tears of joy to the faces in Chicago's Grant Park during president-elect Barack Obama's November 4 acceptance speech? It wasn't just his intellect, poise, oratorical skill, or political acumen. It wasn't even his race. Powerful though those are, I suspect it was his idealism — his articulate conviction that goodness exists, that progress is possible, and that excellence can be attained.

During the campaign, that idealism was never far from the surface. In his acceptance speech it burst forth in his opening sentence, where he talked about an America "where all things are possible" and where "the dream of our founders is alive in our time."

From the outset, it was clear that this speech wasn't going to dwell on wonky policy detail or triumphal political celebration. While he thanked his supporters for his victory, he didn't analyze it. Praising them as people willing to "put their hands on the arc of history and bend it once more toward the hope of a better day," he never told them *how* to do the bending. And when he sought to account for "the true strength of our nation," he traced it not to military prowess or economic might but to "the enduring power of our ideals: democracy, liberty, opportunity, and unyielding hope."

But words are easy. What makes his idealism the sign of a real visionary rather than a mere dreamer? The answer lies in five words, buried deep in his speech, that echo the preamble to the United States Constitution: "Our union can be perfected."

It's a note he's struck before, most notably in his March 18 speech in Philadelphia on the topic of race. There, he mentioned the idea of perfection eleven times. His opening sentence quoted the Constitution's phrase, "a more perfect union." His final sentence ended with the words "where perfection begins." As the faces in Grant Park suggested, this simple conviction — that we can perfect ourselves around a moral ideal — may be the most powerful new force in American politics today.

For Obama, there appears to be nothing unnatural about perfection. That itself is remarkable. In the swirling currents of twenty-first-century thought, the idea that perfection can and should be sought is by no means obvious. We've come through a corrosive half-century of moral relativism, where the ideas of goodness, excellence, and perfection have been severely challenged. To imagine that goodness can exist except as wishful thinking, that excellence has any validity beyond the eye of the beholder, that anything might hope to be made perfect — to a postmodern age, what are these but irrational fancies?

This fashionable skepticism has deep intellectual and religious roots. It appropriates (mistakenly) Albert Einstein's theory of relativity to argue that moral standards are relative, negotiable, and subjective. As for idealism, didn't Bertrand Russell famously describe man's life as "brief and powerless," where "the slow, sure doom falls pitiless and dark" as "omnipotent matter rolls on its relentless way"? And those Biblical beliefs that Obama described in his March 18 speech as having such impact on the black experience — aren't they (ask the skeptics) also suspect? Although the King James Version of the Bible — the translation in use as the Constitution was being written — used the word *perfect* nearly a hundred times, modern Bibles pretty much abandon that word. What eighteenth-century readers heard as "mark the perfect man" becomes, in the New International Version, "consider the blameless," while Jesus's imperative, "be ye therefore perfect," is translated in the Message Bible as "live generously and graciously." Don't we all know, in other words, that our deconstructionist age simply can't bring itself to contemplate the ideal of perfection?

In fact, it seems that Obama *doesn't* know that. For him, perfection is not only worth seeking but is, in its way, attainable. His words give no hint that he regards the perfect as a quaint locution or a creed outworn. He apparently has no interest in settling for a more "blameless" union or even for a more gracious one. Instead, he sees perfection as a core, cutting-edge concept, essential for twenty-first-century political, social, and moral progress.

Which may explain his deep appeal. He's not simply the first black president-elect, nor the first to galvanize such a massive turnout, nor the first to fundraise so effectively on the Internet. He's also the first to reject twentieth-century moral relativism and to speak with authority about the need for perfection — and to watch millions agree.

Does that sense of perfectibility make him perfect? He's not so naïve as to think so. Will it obscure his ability to see and challenge evil? Only if he wrongly assumes that, because perfection is attainable, we're already perfect and don't need to change. What it will provide instead is a basis for authentic, credible idealism — not spangled in hype and oratory, not giddy, glib, or gratuitous, but rooted in a sense of possibility lying beyond the merely probable. Of such conviction strong leadership can be made.

November 10, 2008